Managing the Asian Century

Series editor

Purnendu Mandal, College of Business, Lamar University, Beaumont, TX, USA

Managing the Asian Century provides a platform for scholastic discussions and stresses the need for a holistic framework to understand Asia as an emerging economic global powerhouse. Books published in this series cover Asia-centric topics in economics, production, marketing, finance, entrepreneurship, education, culture, technology, as well as other areas of importance to Asian economics. The series will publish edited volumes based on papers submitted to international and regional conferences that focus on specific Asia-Pacific themes, such as investment in education, women's rights, entrepreneurship, climate change, wage inequality, challenges in governance, and corruption. Books in this series are of keen interest to researchers and policy planners around the world and will be used by universities for graduate and doctoral level studies.

More information about this series at http://www.springer.com/series/13579

Pradip Kumar Ray · Jhareswar Maiti
Editors

Healthcare Systems Management: Methodologies and Applications

21st Century Perspectives of Asia

Springer

Editors
Pradip Kumar Ray
Indian Institute of Technology Kharagpur
Kharagpur
India

Jhareswar Maiti
Indian Institute of Technology Kharagpur
Kharagpur
India

ISSN 2364-5857 ISSN 2364-5865 (electronic)
Managing the Asian Century
ISBN 978-981-10-5630-7 ISBN 978-981-10-5631-4 (eBook)
DOI 10.1007/978-981-10-5631-4

Library of Congress Control Number: 2017945244

Printed on acid-free paper

This Springer imprint is published by Springer Nature
The registered company is Springer Nature Singapore Pte Ltd.
The registered company address is: 152 Beach Road, #21-01/04 Gateway East, Singapore 189721, Singapore

Preface

Healthcare systems, considered an integral part of the socio-economic system of any country, need continuous evaluation and improvement because of their fast-changing technological and resource management systems. In addition to improving its clinical performance as well as overall health condition for well-being of the people, a healthcare system has to meet a number of, often conflicting, operational objectives, such as minimizing the cost of healthcare, maximizing the utilization of physical and human resources, and improving the timeliness of service to the patients. The book addresses the major issues, principles and applications related to healthcare systems management.

This book is a comprehensive text on the Proceedings of the International Conference on Management of Ergonomic Design, Industrial Safety and Healthcare Systems (MESH-2016) held at Indian Institute of Technology Kharagpur, India, during December 20–23, 2016. It is self-contained and the subject matter is presented in an organized and systematic manner. Each chapter in this book consists of a concise but thorough fundamental statement of introduction, methodology and findings followed by results and discussion. The concepts and case studies as presented in the book pertain to the prevailing situations and conditions in Asian countries and their perspectives.

This book is quite appropriate for graduate students, researchers and industrial professionals and can be adapted for a short professional course on the subject matter as well. It is hoped that design and research engineers, willing to learn mathematical models for analytical and design purposes, will be immensely benefited. Also, practicing engineers and managers who want to learn about the basic principles and concepts as applicable to healthcare systems will find the book quite informative and valuable.

Kharagpur, India

Pradip Kumar Ray
Jhareswar Maiti

Contents

Chapter 1
Improving the Performance of an MRI Department Through Appointment Scheduling

P. Bhattacharjee

Abstract Performance management of hospital systems has become extremely crucial due to increasing demand for healthcare services as well as higher expectations in terms of patient satisfaction. There are mainly two different aspects of a hospital system performance, viz. clinical and operational. While the former deals with the effectiveness and appropriateness of treatment, the latter one deals with the proper functioning of the day-to-day operations in a hospital system. For various facilities in a hospital, prior appointments are required to receive the requested service (treatment or investigation). This paper deals with appointment scheduling, which is one of the aspects of improving the operational performance of a hospital system. An example of an MRI department is presented to illustrate the effect of implementing appropriate appointment scheduling rules in an appointment-based hospital system. The trade-off between waiting times of patients and the utilization of the MRI machine is considered for performance analysis.

Keywords Appointment scheduling · Hospital · Performance · Waiting times · Utilization

1.1 Introduction

Healthcare systems being an integral part of the socioeconomic system, need continuous evaluation and improvement because of their fast-changing technological and resource management systems (Brailsford and Vissers 2011). Hospitals are the part of the healthcare system through which the people directly interact with the healthcare system. There may be different types of hospitals, e.g., hospitals may be government hospitals or private hospitals, hospitals may be general hospitals or

---

P. Bhattacharjee (✉)
Decision Sciences Area, Xavier Institute of Management, Bhubaneswar, India
e-mail: papiya@ximb.ac.in

P.K. Ray and J. Maiti (eds.), *Healthcare Systems Management: Methodologies and Applications*, Managing the Asian Century,
DOI 10.1007/978-981-10-5631-4_1

specialized hospitals, etc. A typical hospital is considered as an integrated service unit consisting of several interacting departments (outpatient, inpatient, emergency, pathology, radiology etc.). Among various services provided in a hospital, arrivals of patients are scheduled mainly for the consultation services, investigation and treatment procedure (such as magnetic resonance imaging (MRI), computed tomography (CT) scan, and dialysis), and for surgical services. It is important to continuously evaluate and improve the performance of each unit of a hospital system. Broadly, there are two different aspects of assessing the performance of a hospital unit viz., clinical and operational. Clinical performance is mainly concerned with the effectiveness of care and the overall health condition or well-being of the people (e.g., mortality rate, readmission rate, etc.). Operational Performance mainly assesses the efficiency, utilization and timeliness of a hospital facility. This paper is concerned with the operational performance of a hospital MRI facility. From patients' perspective, the operational performance measure of interest is the waiting time of patients (Kemper et al. 2014; Anderson et al. 2015). From providers' perspective, the operational performance measures of interest may be the utilization and throughput of the facility (Kopach et al. 2007; Jerbi and Kamoun 2011).

It is imperative that operational performance of appointment systems should be modeled under various system conditions and constraints to evaluate the present performance of the system and making improvements through alternate scheduling alternatives. Modeling, analysis and management of patient flows plays a key role in performance evaluation and improvement of hospital systems (Cote 2000; Harper 2002) because direct measurement of the performance of a system under consideration may not always be possible, e.g., during the design phase the actual system does not exist. Moreover, sometimes it is required to evaluate and gain insights about alternative policies intended to be applied to improve the performance, and experimentation with the real system is risky. The congestion in the appointment system may be significantly reduced through a systematic modeling and analysis of patient flows (Marshall et al. 2005; Hall 2006; Zhao and Lie 2008). Through this paper, the benefit of implementing appropriate scheduling rules is illustrated with an illustrative example.

1.2 Appointment Scheduling

Appointment scheduling plays a key role in improving the operational performance and efficiency of a hospital system. Appointment scheduling synchronizes the arrival of patients by allocating particular date and time to receive the service from a particular hospital facility. The goal of appointment scheduling is to find a trade-off between the efficiency of service providers (e.g., maximizing the utilization or minimizing the overtime and idle time of resources, such as physicians, imaging machines and operating rooms, etc.) and satisfaction of patients (e.g., minimizing waiting times, etc.). Any appointment system is a queueing system with scheduled arrivals. The performance of such systems may be evaluated either through queuing theoretic models or through simulation of the patient flows in such systems (Bhattacharjee and Ray 2014).

1.2.1 Appointment Rules

An appointment rule consists of two aspects, the block size (the number patients scheduled at a point in time) and the inter-appointment time. The block size may be individual (only one patient in each block), multiple fixed (multiple but fixed number of patients in each block) or multiple variable (multiple patients in each block, and each block has different number of patients) and the inter-appointment times may be fixed or variable. Various appointment rules have been defined in the literature. The most researched ones are as follows:

1. Individual block fixed interval (IBFI), i.e., one patient is scheduled at equal appointment intervals (e.g., Rohleder and Klassen 2000).
2. Individual block variable interval (IBVI), where inter-arrival times are adjusted according to mean service times of various patient classes.
3. Baily-Welch rule (2BEG), i.e., two patients are scheduled to arrive at the beginning of the session and remaining patients are scheduled at intervals equal to the mean service time of all the patients (originally proposed by Baily 1952).
4. The 2BEGVI rule which is the modification of 2BEG rule where that the inter-appointment times are adjusted per the mean service time of a class of patient.
5. The Multiple Block Fixed Interval rule (MBFI), where two patients are scheduled to arrive in each block, each block being equal to twice the mean service time of the patients (e.g., Liu and Liu 1998).
6. In the Multiple Block Variable Interval (MBVI) rule, two patients are scheduled to arrive in each block, the length of each block being equal to the sum of the mean service times of the two patients scheduled in that block (e.g., Fries and Marathe 1981).
7. In the OFFSET appointment rule, the initial few patents are scheduled close to each other and later the inter-arrival time increases (see Ho and Lau 1992).
8. In the DOME appointment rule, initially the inter-arrival times are short, then increase and again become short (Luo et al. 2012).

1.2.2 Sequencing Rules

Sequencing issues come into picture when there are multiple classes of patients. Sequencing of patient classes in a specific order may help in improving the performance of an appointment system (Cayirli et al. 2006). Patients may be distinct in terms of characteristics, such as arrival rates, service time distribution, mean service time, service time variability, no-show probability and punctuality (Rohleder and Klassen 2000; Vanden Bosch and Dietz 2000; Akin et al. 2013). Other factors for classifying patients, such as investigation/procedure and the source of arrival of patients (outpatients, inpatients, emergency) and priorities based on urgency have also been suggested in the literature (Sickinger and Kolish 2009; Qu et al. 2013). Various sequencing rules have been proposed in the literature. Patients may be scheduled in increasing order of mean service times (shortest processing time or SPT rule) (Wang 1997). Klassen and Rohleder (1996) propose sequencing in increasing order of service time variance/standard deviation. Rules such as alternately sequencing the patients based on mean service time (when there are two classes of patients), i.e., the patients having short service time and those having long service time are scheduled alternately throughout the session; scheduling the patients in such a way that all the patients having short service time are allocated in the middle of the session and patients having long service time are allocated in the beginning and the end or vice versa are also proposed in the literature (Cayirli et al. 2006). There may be several such permutations of classes.

1.3 An Illustration

For illustrating the benefits of using appropriate scheduling rules, an MRI department of a multi-speciality hospital in eastern India is considered. After observing the MRI department and discussing with the concerned personnel, the following details were collected.

1. The MRI department operates for a session length of 12 h per day. However, overtime is allowed to some extent.
2. The patients are scheduled by allotting equidistant inter-appointment times, each time slot being of 40 min (which is considered by the technicians as the average time taken for an MRI scan). In 12 h, at most 18 patients may be given prior appointments in advance at an average time of 40 min per patient. Presently, the patients are considered homogeneous, and are scheduled as first come first served.
3. Usually, less than 18 calls are received in advance (including requests from inpatients), i.e., all the 18 slots are not filled up in advance. However, there are some unscheduled arrivals (walk-ins), i.e., some patients walk-into the Radiology department and request for an investigation to be performed the same day. These are usually those patients who had consultations the same day with physicians at clinics associated with the hospital, and try to get the investigation done on the same visit.
4. Also, there are no-shows among the scheduled outpatients. If a slot is free, the walk-in patient is allotted a slot. Otherwise, the patient is asked to wait for a

no-show or to come later by taking a prior appointment, i.e., the walk-in patients have lower priority of being served than the scheduled patients.
5. The MRI machine keeps functioning till all the scheduled patients get their investigations done or till the session end time (whichever is later).

1.3.1 Performance Analysis of the System

In order to analyze the performance of an appointment system, patient flows are to be modeled. The model should represent the sequencing and appointment rules. Owing to the complexities in patient flows due to multiple classes of patients, unpunctuality and no-shows of scheduled patients and presence of walk-ins and emergency arrivals, discrete-event simulation is used to analyze different scheduling rules. For parameterizing the simulation models, data related to the arrival patterns, punctuality and no-shows of patients and service times in the facility were collected through direct observations and reference to past records of the hospital.

1.3.1.1 Model Conceptualization, Data Collection and Analysis

The MRI appointment system under consideration may be conceptualized by a single node GI/G/1 queue with two classes of scheduled patients (inpatients and outpatients). Additionally, there may be unscheduled low priority walk-in arrivals. Data on arrival patterns, unpunctuality and service times were collected with direct observations and from the log books of the MRI section. Over a period of two months, the relevant data was collected for a sample of 572 patients undergoing various MRI investigations. The service time is defined as the difference in time when a patient enters the MRI room and when the patient exits that room, i.e., it includes the setup time (moving the patient on the table, injecting or feeding the patient with contrast, applying anaesthesia in some instances, etc.) as well as the scanning time.

The number of outpatients (including walk-ins) investigated per day varies from around 55% to 75% (65% on an average) of the total number of patients investigated in a day, and that of inpatients varies from around 25% to 45% (35% on an average) of the total number of patients investigated. The data on arrival patterns reveal that there are unpunctuality and no-shows among the scheduled outpatients. The punctuality level and mean service time for outpatients and inpatients are different. Outpatients are more unpunctual as compared to inpatients as the inpatients are already staying in the hospital, and their arrivals are under the control of hospital staff. The mean service times for outpatients are shorter as compared to that of inpatients, the mean values being 34.8 and 45.9 min respectively. This is because the inpatients usually are less mobile, and need support from relatives or hospital staff to be moved to the investigation room and to lie down on the table. The show-up probability of outpatients is 0.8 and that of inpatients is 1. Inter-arrival times of walk-ins are assumed to follow an exponential distribution with a mean of 60 min. The data for arrival punctuality and service times are analyzed using Arena input analyzer to obtain expressions for the distributions followed by them. It is found that the empirical form of arrival punctuality data does not fit well to any particular theoretical distribution. For our analyses, we assume the punctuality data to follow uniform distribution. The punctuality of scheduled outpatients is assumed to follow a Uniform (−15, 20) distribution and that of inpatients is assumed to follow a Uniform (−10, 10) distribution. The service times are found to follow Beta distributions based on Kolmogorov–Smirnov test at $\alpha = 0.05$. The service time distributions are 12.5 + 54*Beta (1.96, 2.8) and 19.5 + 57*Beta (1.37, 1.59) for outpatients and inpatients respectively. With the arrival punctuality distribution known, we can derive expressions for inter-arrival time distributions. Inter-arrival times for outpatients and inpatients in this case follow Triangular distributions (Ross 1997). Inter-arrival times follow Triangular (5, 40, and 75) and Triangular (20, 40, and 60) distributions for outpatients and inpatients respectively.

1.3.1.2 Classification of Patients

The most common classifications is on the basis of mean service time. For appointment sequencing, the scheduled patients may be classified into two groups (outpatients and inpatients) as these two classes of patients have different mean service times, different levels of punctuality and different show-up probabilities.

1.3.1.3 Performance Analysis

For evaluating the performance of various scheduling rules, we define the average cost of waiting (CW) as follows:

$$\mathrm{CW} = \left\{\sum_{k=1}^{2}(\mathrm{WTk})(\mathrm{NSk}) + \alpha(\mathrm{WTW})\mathrm{NW}\right\} \Big/ \left(\sum_{k=1}^{2}\mathrm{NSk} + \mathrm{NW}\right) \tag{1.1}$$

where, WTk is the average waiting time of scheduled patients of class k and WTW is the average waiting time of walk-in patients given as follows:

$$\mathrm{WTk} = \frac{\sum_{j=1}^{\mathrm{NSk}} \mathrm{WT}_{jk}}{\mathrm{NSk}}, \quad k = 1, 2 \tag{1.2}$$

$$\mathrm{WTW} = \frac{\sum_{m=1}^{\mathrm{NW}} \mathrm{WTW}_m}{\mathrm{NW}} \tag{1.3}$$

NSk is the number of patients of class k served, k = 1, 2; NW is the number of walk-ins served; WT_{jk} is Waiting time of patient j of class k that shows up, j = 1, 2, …,NSk; k = 1, 2; WTW_m is the waiting time of mth walk-in patient; α is the relative cost of waiting per walk-in patient to scheduled patient classes. Cost of waiting may include costs of the elements, such as delayed treatment (there could be additional expenditure on care due to deterioration of health) and cost due to loss of goodwill. On the other hand, cost of underutilization is due to loss of revenue and additional expenditure. Utilization of the facility is given by

$$\begin{aligned} U &= \frac{\text{Total time the service facility is busy}}{\text{Total time the service facility is available}} \times 100 \\ &= \frac{\int_0^{TB} B(t)\mathrm{d}t}{\mathrm{TE}} \times 100 \end{aligned} \tag{1.4}$$

where,

$$B(t) = \begin{cases} 1 & \text{if the facility is busy at time } t \\ 0 & \text{if the facility is idle at time } t \end{cases}$$

TE is Time when the service ends, assuming the session starts at time zero.

1.3.1.4 Model Translation

Simulation software Arena of Rockwell Automation (version 10) (Kelton et al. 2002) is used to simulate/translate the appointment system considered under various combinations of sequencing and appointment rules. Terminating simulation is used for the analysis as the system starts with zero patients (empty system) daily in the morning at the start of the session time and ends as an empty system again when the session ends or all the scheduled patients are served. For analysis of different scheduling rules to be evaluated, a fully loaded system is considered, i.e., all the 18 time slots are allotted/scheduled in advance to the patients (i.e., it is assumed that at least 18 requests for appointments are received). If a walk-in arrives the ith slot, and within 20 min past the starting time of the slot, he/she is forced to wait until 20 min are past from the slot start time. Otherwise, the walk-in may be served immediately if the server is idle. For each of the appointment systems, 1000 independent replications are carried out to ensure that the half-width 95% confidence intervals of the performance measures are less than 5% of the performance estimate.

1.3.1.5 Verification and Validation

All the models are verified to ensure exact representation of the input parameters and proper translation of the system logic. This means that the conceptual model is accurately reflected in the operational model (Banks et al. 2005), and hence reliable output performance measures are assured. For validation of the model of the existing appointment system, the performance of the original system is compared with the results obtained through the simulation model. However, validation of the simulation of appointment systems representing different scheduling rules to be evaluated could not be performed in a similar way as these systems do not really exist.

1.3.1.6 Different Scheduling Systems Evaluated

All the appointment rules described in Sect. 2.1 are evaluated. The sequencing rules that are evaluated are OPBEG (all the outpatients scheduled first and the inpatients are scheduled after the outpatients), IPBEG (the reverse of OPBEG), ALTER (outpatients and inpatients are scheduled alternately), IPOPIP (outpatients are scheduled in the middle of the session), OPIPOP (inpatients are scheduled in the middle of the session).

1.3.2 Results

The performances of sequencing and appointment rules are compared using the efficient frontier of the combined waiting time measure and the utilization measure. The efficient frontier for these two performance helps in visualizing the well-performing sequencing and appointment rules considering a trade-off between the two performance measures. For the values of $\alpha = 0.5$ and $\beta = 1$, the efficient frontiers comparing the sequencing rules using the waiting and utilization

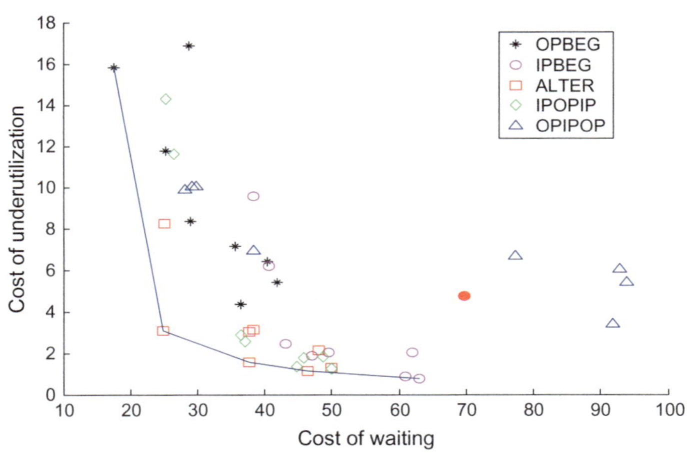

Fig. 1.1 Efficient frontier for cost of waiting and cost of underutilization of MRI machine for inpatient-outpatient classification ($\alpha = 0.5$, $\beta = 1$)

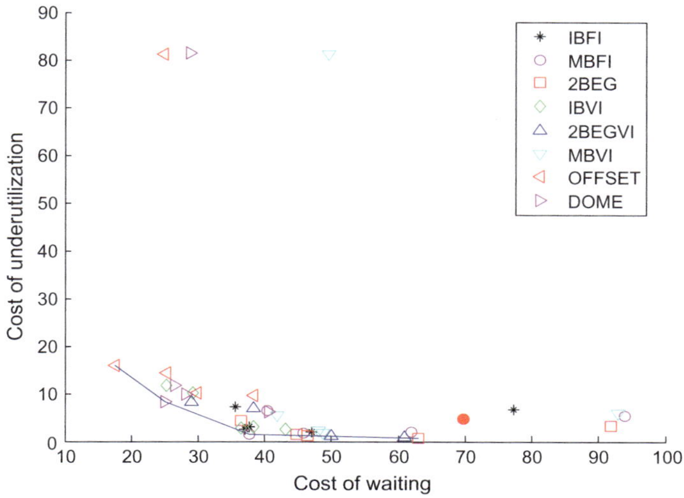

Fig. 1.2 Efficient frontier for cost of waiting and cost of underutilization of MRI machine for inpatient-outpatient classification ($\alpha = 0.5$, $\beta = 1$)

performance measures are given in Fig. 1.1. It is clear that the sequencing rule ALTER dominates all the other sequencing rules followed by the IPOPIP rule. The solid red dot is the current operating point, i.e., it represents the present performance of the system. As the point is far away from the efficient frontier, it is clear that if appropriate sequencing rules are implemented, the performance of the appointment system may be improved significantly. It is seen that the OPIPOP sequencing rule performance even worse than the present appointment system under four of the appointment rules. For other values of α and β, similar results are obtained. From Fig. 1.2, it is seen that the appointment rule IBVI outperforms other appointment rules followed by the OFFSET rule. Again the solid red dot representing the present performance is far away from the efficient frontier.

1.4 Concluding Remarks

In this paper, with the help of an illustrative example, the benefits of implementing appropriate appointment scheduling rules is presented. It is found that significant performance improvements may be achieved through such rules. Timeliness of care/service to patients and utilization of expensive medical equipment are two important aspects of healthcare management. Appointment scheduling takes care of these two aspects, and hence is an important research area in the field of hospital operations management. In this paper, a very simple example has been presented.

Ample research is being carried out in this field throughout the world. Various complexities may be involved in a scheduling problem, such as human preferences, environmental factors and dynamic scheduling.

References

Akin, G., Ivy, J. S., Huschka, T. R., Rohleder, T. R. & Marmor, Y. N. (2013). Capacity management and patient scheduling in an outpatient clinic using discrete event simulation. In R. Pasupathy, S.-H. Kim, A. Tolk, R. Hill & M. E. Kuhl (Eds.), *Proceedings of the 2013 Winter Simulation Conference* (pp. 2215–2226).

Anderson, K., Zheng, B., Won Yoon, S. & Khasawneh, M. T. (2015). An analysis of overlapping appointment scheduling model in an outpatient clinic. Operations Research for Health Care, *4,* 5–14.

Bailey, N. T. J. (1952). A study of queues and appointment systems in hospital out-patient departments, with special reference to waiting-times. *Journal of the Royal Statistical Society, Series B (Methodological), 14*(2), 185–199.

Banks, J., Carson, J. S., Nelson, B. L., & Nicol, D. M. (2005). *Discrete-event system simulation* (4th ed.). USA: Pearson Education Inc.

Bhattacharjee, P. & Ray, P. K. (2014). Patient flow modelling and performance analysis of healthcare delivery processes in hospitals: A review and reflection. Computers and Industrial Engineering, *78,* 299–312.

Brailsford, S., & Vissers, J. (2011). OR in healthcare: A European perspective. *European Journal of Operational Research, 212*(2), 223–234.

Cayirli, T., Veral, E., & Rosen, H. (2006). Designing appointment scheduling systems for ambulatory care services. *Health Care Management Science, 9*(1), 47–58.

Cote, M. J. (2000). Understanding patient flow. *Decision Line, 31,* 8–10.

Fries, B. E., & Marathe, V. P. (1981). Determination of optimal variable sized multiple-block appointment systems. *Operations Research, 29*(2), 324–345.

Hall, R. W. (Ed.). (2006). *Patient flow: Reducing delay in healthcare delivery*. USA: Springer-Verlag.

Harper, P. R. (2002). A framework for operational modelling of hospital resources. *Health Care Management Science, 5*(3), 165–173.

Ho, C., & Lau, H. (1992). Minimizing total cost in scheduling outpatient appointments. *Management Science, 38*(12), 1750–1764.

Jerbi, B., & Kamoun, H. (2011). Multiobjective study to implement outpatient appointment system at Hedi Chaker Hospital. *Simulation Modelling Practice and Theory, 19*(5), 1363–1370.

Kelton, D., Sadowski, R., & Sadowski, D. (2002). *Simulation with Arena*. New York, NY: McGraw-Hill.

Kemper, B., Klaasen, C. A. J., & Mandjes, M. (2014). Optimized appointment scheduling. *European Journal of Operational Research, 239*(1), 243–255.

Klassen, K. J., & Rohleder, T. R. (1996). Scheduling outpatient appointments in a dynamic environment. *Journal of Operations Management, 14*(2), 83–101.

Kopach, R., DeLaurentis, P. C., Lawley, M., Muthuraman, K., Ozsen, L., Rardin, R., et al. (2007). Effects of clinical characteristics on successful open access scheduling. *Health Care Management Science, 10*(2), 111–124.

Liu, L., & Liu, X. (1998). Block appointment systems for outpatient clinics with multiple doctors. *Journal of the Operational Research Society, 49*(12), 1254–1259.

Luo, J., Kulkarni, V. G., & Ziya, S. (2012). Appointment scheduling under patient no-shows and service interruptions. *Manufacturing and Service Operations Management, 14*(4), 670–684.

Marshall, A., Vasilakis, C., & El-Darzi, E. (2005). Length of stay-based patient flow models: Recent developments and future directions. *Health Care Management Science, 8*(3), 213–220.
Qu, X., Peng, Y., Kong, N., & Shi, J. (2013). A two-phase approach to scheduling multi-category outpatient appointments–a case study of a women's clinic. *Health Care Management Science,* 16(3), 197–216.
Rohleder, T. R., & Klassen, K. J. (2000). Using client-variance information to improve dynamic appointment scheduling performance. *Omega, 5*(3), 201–209.
Ross, M. (1997). *Introduction to probability models* (7th ed.). San Diego: Academic Press.
Sickinger, S., & Kolisch, R. (2009). The performance of a generalized Bailey-Welch rule for outpatient appointment scheduling under inpatient and emergency demand. *Health Care Management Science, 12*(4), 408–419.
Vanden Bosch, P. M., & Dietz, C. D. (2000). Minimizing expected waiting in a medical appointment system. *IIE Transactions, 32*(9), 841–848.
Wang, P. P. (1997). Optimally scheduling N customer arrival times for a single-server system. *Computers and Operations Research, 24*(8), 703–716.
Zhao, L. & Lie, B. (2008), Modeling and simulation of patient flow in hospitals for resource utilization. In *Proceedings of 49th Scandinavian Conference on Simulation and Modeling*. Oslo University college.

Chapter 2
Measurement of Efficiency and Productivity Growth of Hospital Systems: A Indian Case Study

Abhik Patra and Pradip Kumar Ray

Abstract The increased importance of the healthcare sector over the last two decades and current concern over productivity growth have stirred interest in productivity and efficiency measures in this expanding sector of the economic system. Productivity in economic position is determined as the relation between output and input. Productivity concept in manufacturing is analysed in the scope of the organization, but in the service sector like in hospital, this arena is larger and needs an external portion of the organizational position as patients. This paper deals with the measurement of efficiency and productivity growth of the hospital systems. To measure productivity and efficiency of an Indian hospital system, the Malmquist productivity index is applied, based on the data envelopment analysis (DEA). The efficiency and productivity of several departments of the given hospital are analysed and the improvement alternatives also identified.

Keywords Hospital system · Malmquist productivity index · Data envelopment analysis

2.1 Introduction

Over the past two decades, the healthcare sector in general and hospital systems, in particular, have experienced notable advancements in the field of health service operation and technological alignment. Even so, the gain in health service productivity cannot be captured by the Bureau of Labour Statistics (BLS) (Chansky et al. 2016). As the service function, the hospital system may face the difficulty in the measurement of its productivity as well as its efficiency because of the conflation in the input and output, inherent in any service function (Rosenstein 1991). With increasing health service costs, there has been utmost concerned by the

---

A. Patra (✉) · P.K. Ray
Department of Industrial and Systems Engineering, IIT Kharagpur, 721302 Kharagpur, India
e-mail: abhikpatra@iitkgp.ac.in

P.K. Ray and J. Maiti (eds.), *Healthcare Systems Management: Methodologies and Applications*, Managing the Asian Century,
DOI 10.1007/978-981-10-5631-4_2

government of the developed as well as developing countries about the productivity and the efficiency of the hospital systems (Chang et al. 2011). Inefficient utilization of the resources is a major reason for the exaggerated healthcare cost (Walker and Dunn 2006). Hence, the efficient and cost-effective healthcare service delivery in the hospital organization has contributed to more efficient analysis and monitoring about the rule of the hospital productivity (Prior 2006). As a complex system, with combination of multiple inputs and outputs, hospital productivity may show some pattern with the determining factors. Thus, to distinguish the trends of hospital productivity as a whole or for any particular department, analytical approach has to be used.

In this chapter, a Malmquist output-based productivity index is applied to an Indian hospital system to identify the productivity pattern of the hospital and to analyse its relationship with other determining factors. In this study, output distance functions are employed to construct the Malmquist productivity index (MPI), established on the constant returns to scale output-oriented data envelopment analysis (DEA) model to evaluate the hospital productivity.

2.2 DEA and Malmquist Productivity Index-Based Methodology

The hospital system, as a complex service function is extremely mixed with various inspection and service units that are offered to match the needs of the patients. The typical hospital system is the combination of various interacting departments and sub-units such as Outpatient Department (OPD), Emergency Department, Inpatient Department, Operating Theatre (OT), Department of Pathology, Radiology Department, etc., within a specified area. Every department has some predefined responsibility. Referable to the integrity of the hospital system, every department is shared with some problems, such as a resource constraint, physician and facility availability, etc. Hence it is imperative to measure the operational efficiency and productivity of the select department with respect to system constraints. Overall performance of the hospital system is purely dependent on the operational efficiency and productivity of all departments.

For measuring productivity of a hospital system, the productivity index as proposed by Malmquist (1953) is recommended to be used. The Malmquist productivity index measures the changes in total factor productivity (TFP) between two data points in terms of ratios of distance functions (Caves et al. 1982). The computation of the Malmquist productivity index is based on the use of a nonparametric method, called data envelopment analysis [DEA]. DEA is an abstraction of the nonparametric method of productivity measurement (Farrell 1957). As per this approach, the proposed measure of the efficiency of any hospital is obtained as the upper limit of a ratio of weighted outputs to weighted inputs subject to the conditions that the similar ratios for every hospital be less than or equal to unity (Charnes et al. 1978). The problem is formulated as

$$\text{Maximize } Q_0 = \frac{\sum_{r=1}^{s} u_r y_{r0}}{\sum_{i=1}^{m} v_i x_{i0}}. \tag{2.1}$$

$$\text{subject to } \frac{\sum_{r=1}^{s} u_r y_{rj}}{\sum_{i=1}^{m} v_i x_{ij}} \leq 1$$

u_r, $v_i \geq 0$ for all r and i,

where Q_0 is the efficiency scores, the number of output r from hospital department j (y_{rj}, r = 1,…, s) and the number of input i from hospital department j (x_{ij}, i = 1,…, m). u_r and v_i are the weights for the outputs and inputs, respectively.

The efficiency of any department is measured by the relative efficiency of the set of departments (j = 1,…, n). The subscript, o represents the optimization of the objective function as well as for the constraints that indicate the maximization of the hospital department efficiency with the maximum favourable weights that the constraints permit.

The DEA methodology identifies the best practice production frontier piecewise linear function, where observed data points lie on or below that frontier (Hollingsworth 2003). The efficiency of a department is measured based on the virtual relative efficient department determined as a weighted average of the real efficient departments, and used as a comparative unit for the other departments. The virtual efficient unit is imputed from the linear combination of the inputs and outputs of the single or multiple efficient service units.

Mathematical formation of the DEA approach represents as a ratio of the weighted output and input, that should be maximized, and each constraint represents the specific hospital department reflecting the virtual inputs and outputs of the department that should be less than or equal to one. The efficient production function and efficiency score for each of the combined hospital's department are determined by solving that linear programing problem of DEA methodology where efficiency of the combined department is measured in terms of outputs.

In the DEA approach, ratio of the weighted output and input of the production or service unit is used to measure the efficiency of the respective production function. The efficiency of the hospital department is measured in terms of increase in the output vectors or decrease in the input vectors, with respect to best performing department (Chakraborty et al. 2001). For productive efficiency, calculation of the government-run organizations or nonprofit organizations, like hospital system where standard price for the output is not available, DEA has been applied very often (Sengupta 1998). DEA-based approach not only gives the efficiency score of the production or service unit but also gives the insight about the improvement alternatives for the decision-makers and practitioners, under such circumstances. DEA is considered as a better approach compared to the ratio analysis or the regression analysis (Liu et al. 2004).

The Malmquist productivity index evaluates the total factor productivity difference between two data points in terms of the ratios of distance functions. The change in the output-oriented Malmquist total factor productivity between the periods, t and $t + 1$ is defined as (Farrell 1957)

$$M_o^{t,t+1}(x^t, y^t, x^{t+1}, y^{t+1}) = \left[\frac{D_o^{t+1}(x^{t+1}, y^{t+1}) \times D_o^t(x^{t+1}, y^{t+1})}{D_o^t(x^t, y^t) \times D_o^{t+1}(x^t, y^t)}\right]^{1/2} \quad (2.2)$$

where, D_o is the distance functions, y the output, x the input, t the time period and M_o the productivity factor.

The Malmquist index is expressed as the square root of the product of two indices evaluating the productivity change by measuring the ratio of distance functions grounded on the same technology for two input output functions between two successive periods. In case, the second period is evaluated with a lower distance than the first period, with an index below unity, a decrease in productivity is indicated (Zere 2000). Similarly, a value greater than unity indicates improvement in productivity. The Malmquist index is the average of two indices based on the technologies being used during a particular periods (Pilyavsky and Staat 2008).

The MPI is additionally decomposed into two parts: one measuring efficiency change and the other measuring technological change (Färe et al. 1994). The decomposition procedure is given below.

$$M_o^{t,t+1}(x^t, y^t, x^{t+1}, y^{t+1}) = \left[\frac{D_o^{t+1}(x^{t+1}, y^{t+1})}{D_o^t(x^t, y^t)}\right]\left[\frac{D_o^t(x^t, y^t) \times D_o^t(x^{t+1}, y^{t+1})}{D_o^{t+1}(x^t, y^t) \times D_o^{t+1}(x^{t+1}, y^{t+1})}\right]^{1/2} \quad (2.3)$$

The first right-hand side part of the Eq. (2.3) measures efficiency change and the second part measures technical change. This part can be expressed as an index for efficiency change (Färe et al. 1994):

$$\Delta\, Efficiency = \left[\frac{D_o^{t+1}(x^{t+1}, y^{t+1})}{D_o^t(x^t, y^t)}\right] \quad (2.4)$$

Equation (2.4) represents the ratio of the two input and output distance functions between two successive periods, each of the ratio score representing the technology change of the corresponding period. It is apparent that a value more than unity indicates an increasing trend in individual efficiency. The index for technical change (Farrell 1957) is expressed as

$$\Delta\, Technology = \left[\frac{D_o^t(x^t, y^t) \times D_o^t(x^{t+1}, y^{t+1})}{D_o^{t+1}(x^t, y^t) \times D_o^{t+1}(x^{t+1}, y^{t+1})}\right]^{1/2} \quad (2.5)$$

where it is assumed that $M_o(t, t + 1) = \Delta\text{Efficiency} \times \Delta\text{Technology}$. ΔTechnology is the square root of the artefact of two indices calculated as the ratio of the distance functions. In this study, the same input output function is benchmarked with respect to two different technologies. For example, the selected function is evaluated as more efficient when benchmarked with a technology from an earlier period instead of with the technology from a later period, because of technological advancements. Therefore, all values of indices greater than unity indicate an advancement.

2.3 Data Collection

The relevant data are collected from a select Hospital located in Eastern India for a period of 4 months (December '15–March '16). For the productivity and efficiency analysis of the given hospital system, the details of operations of the hospital system are studied. As the ideal output and input may be measuring, conceptually as well as empirically, whereas the numbers of physicians and nurses are considered as inputs and the number of patients is considered as the output. As of data is to be collected in limited by their availability. Only one type of output is considered in the study as first approximation. Various operational data, such as the number of patients attended in the respective departments, the number of physicians and registered nurses are collected from the given hospital system. The data from the various departments are combined and added for the easy evaluation of the measures. For examples, the term SEE means the combination of skin, eye and ENT clinic, OCD means the combination of orthopaedic, chest and the dental clinic, PG means the combination of paediatric and gynaecology clinic, MSP means the combination of medicine, surgery and psychiatric clinic, etc. It is observed that there is a growth in number of patients attended in the following departments from December '15 to March '16, viz., in Skin clinic 12.44%, Eye clinic 15.75%, Orthopaedic clinic 48.88%, Dental clinic 90.84%, Paediatric clinic 20.56%, Medicine clinic 15.08%, Psychiatric clinic 70.83% whereas the number of patients attended in ENT clinic and Chest clinic decreased by 7.43 and 51.61%, respectively.

2.4 Results and Discussion

By the DEA method, the technical efficiency of the combined department of the given hospital is determined. The results as obtained are given in Table 2.1. It can be seen that the combination of skin, eye and ENT clinic (SEE) has the lowest average technical efficiency as compared to the other combined departments. Higher number of physicians and nurses employed (input) in the department as compared to other departments is the main reason of lower technical efficiency. The combination of paediatric and gynaecology clinic (PG) has the highest technical efficiency as compared to the other combined departments as the number of physicians and nurses employed (input) is lower than other departments.

Table 2.1 Efficiency of the combined departments calculated by DEA Method

Combined departments	Efficiency calculated by DEA method in the month			
	December '15	January '16	February '16	March '16
SEE	0.720	0.7488	0.754	0.657
OCD	0.746	1	1	1
PG	1	1	1	0.9124
MSP	0.8425	0.9427	0.8838	1

Table 2.2 Malmquist productivity indexes for hospital departments from December '15 to March '16

Departments	January '16/December '15	February '16/January '16	March '16/February '16	Average
SEE	1.297	0.982	0.853	1.044
OCD	1.67	0.975	0.979	1.208
PG	1.14	1.06	0.821	1.007
MSP	1.276	0.998	1.018	1.097
Average	1.3457	1.0037	0.9177	1.089

The results indicate relative differences in the efficiency of the analysed departments of the given hospital. As has been observed, a score of one for a department does not necessarily mean that it has the potential to perform. It may also imply that no linear combination of the other departments in the hospital, as a combined unit, can raise at least as much output as may be obtained from the individual input using the same or less input. Hence, it is improbable to conclude that the departments achieving efficiency at the level of 1 are considered effective all the time.

The result pertaining to changes in productivity over time for different combinations of the departments considered as well as for the entire hospital, and the corresponding values of Malmquist index are listed in Table 2.2. It is observed that the maximum productivity change has occurred during the period December '15–January '16 (34.57% increase in productivity noted in January '16 compared to the previous month). However, in March '16 there had been a productivity decrease of 8.23% as compared to the previous month.

The Malmquist index is applied to find out both the technological (movement of production function) as well as the technical efficiency change. The results are presented in Tables 2.3 and 2.4. It is observed that the technological change had been most significant during the period of December '15–January '16 and minimum during February '16–March '16.

Table 2.3 Technological change of the hospital departments in the period December '15–March '16

Departments	January '16/December '15	February '16/January '16	March '16/February '16
SEE	1.141	1.065	0.9
OCD	1.139	1.065	0.9
PG	1.14	1.06	0.89
MSP	1.14	1.064	0.9

Table 2.4 Efficiency change of the Hospital Departments in the period December '13–March '14

Departments	January '16/December '15	February '16/January '16	March '16/February '16
SEE	1.1366	0.922	0.947
OCD	1.466	0.915	1.087
PG	1	1	0.9124
MSP	1.119	0.9373	1.131

2.5 Conclusion

Since healthcare resources may be considering exceedingly scarce, it is of interest to find out if any significant deviations in the efficiency of healthcare providers can be noticed. The results as obtained through the study throw light on the productivity changes as occurring in a number of hospital departments. Outcomes indicate that there has been a real step-up in productivity during the period, December '15–January '16 and a decrease in productivity during period, February '16–March '16. As the combination of skin, eye and ENT department in particular has the lowest efficiency compared to other combined departments. Performance of skin, eye and ENT (SEE) clinics need improvement. There has also been significant in the value of technology factors indicative of significant effect of technological changes as productivity of the hospital systems.

As a future work, data from other hospitals can be collected and the select hospital can be compared to other hospitals on the basis of productivity and efficiency. Productivity and efficiency of the inpatient department of the hospital can also be valued following the combined DEA-Malmquist productivity index methodology. The relationship between the quality of the healthcare systems and the productivity of hospital system resources for different can also be explored following the proposed methodology.

Appendices

LINGO Codes for distance ratios

The codes are depicted for the SEE and OCD department for the period of January '16/December '15 and February '16/January '16 the codes for the repose of the department and for the period March '16/February '16 is similarly managed with the data adjusted with the respective stops and the departments as per the data collection. Malmquist productivity index, the technological change and the technical efficiency change can be computed by the distance ratios which will be figured by passing the following codes.

SEE

	January '16/December '15	February '16/January '16
Do(t + 1) [x(t + 1), y(t + 1)]	MIN = x; a*(3 + 4) + b*(3 + 4) + c*(2 + 2) + d*(3 + 3) ≤ x*(3 + 4); a*659 + b*880 + c*536 + d*758 ≥ 659; a ≥ 0; b ≥ 0; c ≥ 0; d ≥ 0;	MIN = x; a*(3 + 4) + b*(3 + 4) + c*(2 + 2) + d*(3 + 3) ≤ x*(3 + 4); a*647 + b*858 + c*571 + d*757 ≥ 858; a ≥ 0; b ≥ 0; c ≥ 0; d ≥ 0;
Do(t)[x (t + 1),y (t + 1)]	MIN = x; a*(3 + 4) + b*(3 + 4) + c*(2 + 2) + d*(3 + 3) ≤ x*(3 + 4); a*508 + b*526 + c*470 + d*594 ≥ 659; a ≥ 0; b ≥ 0; c ≥ 0; d ≥ 0;	MIN = x; a*(3 + 4) + b*(3 + 4) + c*(2 + 2) + d*(3 + 3) ≤x*(3 + 4); a*659 + b*880 + c*536 + d*758 ≥ 647; a ≥ 0; b ≥ 0; c ≥ 0; d ≥ 0;
Do(t + 1) [x(t),y(t)]	MIN = x; a*(3 + 4) + b*(3 + 4) + c*(2 + 2) + d*(3 + 3) ≤ x*(3 + 4); a*659 + b*880 + c*536 + d*758 ≥ 508; a ≥ 0; b ≥ 0; c ≥ 0; d ≥ 0;	MIN = x; a*(3 + 4) + b*(3 + 4) + c*(2 + 2) + d*(3 + 3) ≤ x*(3 + 4); a*647 + b*858 + c*571 + d*757 ≥ 659; a ≥ 0; b ≥ 0; c ≥ 0; d ≥ 0;
Do(t)[x(t), y(t)]	MIN = x; a*(3 + 4) + b*(3 + 4) + c*(2 + 2) + d*(3 + 3) ≤ x*(3 + 4); a*508 + b*526 + c*470 + d*594 ≥ 508; a ≥ 0; b ≥ 0; c ≥ 0; d ≥ 0;	MIN = x; a*(3 + 4) + b*(3 + 4) + c*(2 + 2) + d*(3 + 3) ≤ x*(3 + 4); a*659 + b*880 + c*536 + d*758 ≥ 659; a ≥ 0; b ≥ 0; c ≥ 0; d ≥ 0;

OCD

	January '16/December '15	February '16/January '16
Do(t + 1) [x(t + 1), y(t + 1)]	MIN = x; a*(3 + 4) + b*(3 + 4) + c*(2 + 2) + d* (3 + 3) ≤ x*(3 + 4); a*659 + b*880 + c*536 + d*758 ≥ 880; a ≥ 0; b ≥ 0; c ≥ 0; d ≥ 0;	MIN = x; a*(3 + 4) + b*(3 + 4) + c*(2 + 2) + d* (3 + 3) ≤ x*(3 + 4); a*647 + b*858 + c*571 + d*757 ≥ 858; a ≥ 0; b ≥ 0; c ≥ 0; d ≥ 0;
Do(t) [x(t + 1), y(t + 1)]	MIN = x; a*(3 + 4) + b*(3 + 4) + c*(2 + 2) + d* (3 + 3) ≤ x*(3 + 4); a*508 + b*526 + c*470 + d*594 ≥ 880; a ≥ 0; b ≥ 0; c ≥ 0; d ≥ 0;	MIN = x; a*(3 + 4) + b*(3 + 4) + c*(2 + 2) + d* (3 + 3) ≤ x*(3 + 4); a*659 + b*880 + c*536 + d*758 ≥ 858; a ≥ 0; b ≥ 0; c ≥ 0; d ≥ 0;
Do(t + 1) [x(t),y(t)]	MIN = x; a*(3 + 4) + b*(3 + 4) + c*(2 + 2) + d* (3 + 3) ≤ x*(3 + 4); a*659 + b*880 + c*536 + d*758 ≥ 526; a ≥ 0; b ≥ 0; c ≥ 0; d ≥ 0;	MIN = x; a*(3 + 4) + b*(3 + 4) + c*(2 + 2) + d* (3 + 3) ≤ x*(3 + 4); a*647 + b*858 + c*571 + d*757 ≥ 880; a ≥ 0; b ≥ 0; c ≥ 0; d ≥ 0;
Do(t)[x(t), y(t)]	MIN = x; a*(3 + 4) + b*(3 + 4) + c*(2 + 2) + d* (3 + 3) ≤ x*(3 + 4); a*508 + b*526 + c*470 + d*594 ≥ 526; a ≥ 0; b ≥ 0; c ≥ 0; d ≥ 0;	MIN = x; a*(3 + 4) + b*(3 + 4) + c*(2 + 2) + d* (3 + 3) ≤ x*(3 + 4); a*659 + b*880 + c*536 + d*758 ≥ 880; a ≥ 0; b ≥ 0; c ≥ 0; d ≥ 0;

References

Chansky, B., Garner, C., & Raichoudhary, R. (2016). Measuring output and productivity in private hospitals. In *Measuring and modeling health care costs*. University of Chicago Press.

Rosenstein, A. (1991). Health economics and resource management: A model for hospital efficiency. *Hospital and Health Services Administration, 36,* 313–330.

Chang, S. J., Hsiao, H. C., Huang, L. H., & Chang, H. (2011). Taiwan quality indicator project and hospital productivity growth. *Omega, 39*(1), 14–22.

Walker, K. B., & Dunn, L. M. (2006). Improving hospital performance and productivity with the balanced scorecard. *Academy of Health Care Management Journal, 2,* 85–110.

Prior, D. (2006). Efficiency and total quality management in health care organizations: A dynamic frontier approach. *Annals of Operations Research, 145,* 281–299.

Malmquist, S. (1953). Index numbers and indifference surfaces. *Trabajos de estadística, 4*(2), 209–242.

Caves, D. W., Christensen, L. R., & Diewert, W. E. (1982). The economic theory of index numbers and the measurement of input, output, and productivity. *Econometrica*: *Journal of the Econometric Society*, 1393–1414.

Farrell, M. J. (1957). The measurement of productive efficiency. *Journal of the Royal Statistical Society*. Series A (General), *120*(3), 253–290.

Charnes, A., Cooper, W. W., & Rhodes, E. (1978). Measuring the efficiency of decision making units. *European Journal of Operational Research, 2*(6), 429–444.

Hollingsworth, B. (2003). Non-parametric and parametric applications measuring efficiency in health care. *Health Care Management Science, 6*(4), 203–218.

Chakraborty, K., Biswas, B., & Lewis, W. C. (2001). Measurement of technical efficiency in public education: A stochastic and non-stochastic production function approach. *Southern Economic Journal*, 889–905.

Sengupta, J. K. (1998). Testing allocative efficiency by data envelopment analysis. *Applied Economics Letters, 5,* 689–692.

Liu, C., Jung, C., & Chen. C. (2004). Incorporating value judgments into data envelopment analysis to improve decision quality for organization. *Journal of American Academy of Business*, Cambridge, 423–434.

Zere, E. (2000). *Hospital efficiency in Sub-Saharan Africa*. Working papers No 187, UNU World Institute for Development Economics Research, p. 48.

Pilyavsky, A., & Staat, M. (2008). Efficiency and productivity change in Ukrainian health care. *Journal of Productivity Analysis, 29*(2), 143–154.

Färe, R., Grosskopf, S., Lindgren, B., & Roos, P. (1994). Productivity developments in Swedish hospitals: A Malmquist output index approach. In *Data envelopment analysis: Theory, Methodology, and Applications* (pp. 253–272). Netherlands: Springer.

Chapter 3
Integrated Trauma Management System

**Gopinath Chattopadhyay, Michael Schuetz, Gour Karmakar,
Sandeep Halder, Stephen Rashford, Young-Jin Oh
and Sanjay Mishra**

Abstract Trauma has a huge impact on the society and the economy. Large distances between the various human settlements in Queensland are a major challenge for the delivery of desired trauma care. In addition, health care budget has been struggling due to staggering costs. An integrated trauma management system (ITMS) is expected to maximise the appropriate and judicious use of available resources and deliver best possible services within budget constraints. A limited number of researches have been conducted to identify resource constraints and effective diversions for trauma cases in remote parts of Queensland. ITMS proposed in this paper covers activities, events and persons involved in trauma management. It analyses the impact of resource constraints and diversion rules for effective trauma care. Pre-hospital data are used for developing a process map. Simulation using Queensland scenarios assumed patients arrivals following the referral from

G. Chattopadhyay (✉) · G. Karmakar
Federation University, Ballarat, Australia
e-mail: g.chattopadhyay@federation.edu.au

G. Karmakar
e-mail: gour.karmakar@federation.edu.au

M. Schuetz
Queensland University of Technology, Brisbane, Australia
e-mail: m.schuetz@qut.edu.au

S. Halder
RG Kar Medical College and Hospital, Kolkata, India
e-mail: hsandip@yahoo.com

S. Rashford
Emergency Services Complex, Brisbane, Australia
e-mail: Stephen.Rashford@dcs.qld.gov.au

Y.-J. Oh
Sangji University, Wonju, Republic of Korea
e-mail: ooyyjj@sangji.ac.kr

S. Mishra
Department of Science and Technology, New Delhi, India
e-mail: sanjaykr.mishra@nic.in

P.K. Ray and J. Maiti (eds.), *Healthcare Systems Management: Methodologies and Applications*, Managing the Asian Century,
DOI 10.1007/978-981-10-5631-4_3

regional/remote hospitals to regional trauma centres and to major trauma centres. Time stamps are used for the development and analysis of a simulation model using probabilistic approach for time to definitive care and patient outcomes. ITMS is able to further enhance quality of strategic planning. It can be extended to real time decision-making for better healthcare and reducing delays for arriving at definitive care. It is expected to further improve clinical outcome and transform the existing healthcare system into a more efficient, cost-effective and high quality healthcare service to the people living in remote areas.

Keywords Integrated model · Trauma Management Systems · Major injury cases

3.1 Introduction

Trauma is defined as physical damage or harm to the body as a result of exposure to environmental, social or behavioural determinants. Trauma is one of the major causes of mortality, morbidity and disability in younger generation in Australia and New Zealand. Advanced Trauma Life Support (ATLS) training programme for doctors and the paramedics for the management of acute trauma cases was developed by the American College of Surgeons in 1980 (American College of Surgeons 2016). The Royal Australasian College of Surgeons (RACS) has a strong history in trauma care (Royal Australian College of Surgeons 2016). The Early Management of Severe Trauma (EMST) course was developed for setting standards. Coordinated efforts of various health and related organisations have contributed substantially to the clinical care, patient transfer and education of the health professionals to reduce the mortality and morbidity. In 2007, 716 accidents deaths were accounted that is equivalent to 2.8% of all registered deaths of Queenslanders. Costs to the Queensland economy was an estimated $4.013 billion with more than 1500 deaths each year (Australian Bureau of Statistics 2016). The leading causes are: falls (28%); motor vehicle accidents (20%), struck by/against objects (19%) and assaults (11%). Trauma contributes to more than 60% of the ambulance calls. It has a huge socio-economic impact (Fitzgerald et al. 2006, 2008). Complex and major traumatic injury can lead to economic burden to the individual patients, families and the society as a whole (Worthington 1991). This becomes more of a challenge for regional Queensland where distance is huge. Studies are limited to planning Emergency Department. None of the studies had considered an integrated model over a large area (such as Queensland) and reducing the waiting time for definite care using resource as a decision variable.

The response time and coverage rate are regarded as the most influential factors for improving survival rate especially for cardiac arrest patients (Thi Nguyen 2015). Emergency Medical Services (EMS) are classified into two areas—(i) strategic planning (Yang et al. 2016) and (ii) tactic and operational (Lei et al. 2015; Chen et al. 2013) planning. The strategic planning looks at longer term view (e.g. the number of stations and their locations, and the location and allocation of an emergency vehicle) to provide better quality of life without considering the changing factors of a system and its environment, while the tactic and operational planning configures the system considering on-demand requests and dynamic changes based on the status and location of an emergency vehicle; the road, weather and traffic conditions; and the expertise of the care providers and quality of service and facility departments. A decision support system is usually developed by applying queuing theory (Worthington 1987), probabilistic model, integer programing (Lei et al. 2015), simulation modelling (Meadows et al. 2013) and a hybrid amongst them (Butler et al. 1992). Daskin et al. (2004) used accessibility, adaptability and availability in the location planning for a health care system. As strategic planning is of paramount importance to estimate the resources and their cost effectiveness to cope with the future demands. A simulation model developed by a machine learning technique using historical data and the relevant information of application domains (e.g. health care, traffic management, finance) is used for planning. An ITMS is able to further enhance quality in decision-making.

Our proposed ITMS includes the description of the activities, events resources needed for trauma care. It considers date and time of initiation and completion of an activity, actual and estimated duration of those activities, start point and endpoint of travel using locations, postcodes and GPS for distances, risk assessments and estimates delays between time stamps in the transfer and care processes.

The outline of this paper is: in Sect. 3.1, an introduction of Trauma Management Systems and literature research are provided. Following this introduction, Sect. 3.2 provides an overview of the proposed system. The proposed system is analysed with illustrative examples in Sect. 3.3. Finally, conclusion is provided in Sect. 3.4.

3.2 Proposed System

While proposing an integrated system for trauma management, a number of factors, such as types of data, standard practice, resources and location of trauma clinics are considered. The following data are considered:

Availability of beds/personnel in emergency departments, trauma units and surgical units in Queensland, diverted ambulance to other facilities or units due to non-availability of bed or staff or resources at the original destination, ambulance/Helicopter/Jet plane for emergency service, Royal Flying Doctor Service (RFDS), cancelled/rescheduled surgeries in a normal trauma unit due to emergency cases, non-availability of beds/personnel or both and/or designated trauma theatre.

The standard practice is related to the following issues:

(a) Nurse: Patient ratio in a general hospital and for emergency and trauma facility.
(b) Hospital occupancy ratio and availability of vacant beds, resources for a major emergency or disaster scenario.
(c) Variation in arrival rate of trauma cases due to time of the day or night, day of the week, public holidays, long weekend and school holidays, weather condition, dry and wet.

The resources considered are of the following types:

Number of beds in a trauma clinic, number of staff, nurses, paramedics and doctors at each facility, infrastructure, X-ray, CT/MRI, Pathology, Blood Bank, Intensive Therapy Unit, general surgeon, neurosurgeon, anaesthetist and radiologist

Location of trauma clinics is to be defined in the following ways:

Level of trauma centre with required manpower and infrastructure, trauma clinic intermediate level, trauma clinic of basic nature with minimum basic facility, trained personnel in society/work place health and safety.

Additionally, factors like services available in a hospital set up, fixed and variable costs, health care resources at private and government sector, Education and training (EMST) are also to be considered.

3.2.1 Background

Queensland is the second largest state of Australia with a geographical size of 1.7 million square kilometres and population of 4.72 million. The population of this state is concentrated in South East Queensland which is Brisbane, Logan city, Redland, Ipswich, Gold Coast, Sunshine Coast and Toowoomba. Regional centres are Cairns, Mt Isa, Townsville, Mackay, Rockhampton, Bundaberg and Harvey Bay (Australian Bureau of Statistics 2016). There may be a considerable delay in the location where an injury occurs, and risk of death and mobility or disability is twice if accident happens in rural area compared to metropolitan city (Royal Australian College of Surgeons 2016). The patients in remote area are facing complex issues including long distance to travel, limited local resources and communication problems, non-availability of resources for transfer of the patients, shortage of experienced attendant for the inter-hospital transfers, delays in the dispatch of air ambulances and shortage of appropriate accompanying physicians during the inter-hospital transfers (Australian Bureau of Statistics 2016; Australian Government 2016). The hospitals in Queensland for trauma management are identified with post codes and the locations (About Australia 2016).

Hospital systems for Trauma management in Queensland are as follows (FitzGerald et al. 2006):

Major Trauma Services (MTS): It is the hub of an integrated system, a 24 h trauma reception team, on-site neurosurgery, cardiothoracic surgery, intensive care facilities in addition to the other specialist resources. It delivers definitive care to the majority of patients with complex and severe injuries. In Queensland this service is available in Royal Brisbane and Women's Hospital (RBWH), Princess Alexandra Hospital (PAH) and Townsville Hospital (TTH). Majority of the paediatric major trauma services are based at the Royal Children's Hospital.

Metropolitan and *Regional Trauma Services* (MRTS): This service would manage mainly complex injured patients who cannot be optimally managed by Primary Injury Service or by Primary Health Service and need not require the care by MTS.

(i) Metropolitan Trauma Services are available in Ipswich Hospital, Logan Hospital, Mater Hospital, Redcliffe and Caboolture Hospital in Queensland.
(ii) Regional Trauma Services are available at Cairns Base Hospital, Mackay Base Hospital, Rockhampton Base Hospital, Harvey Bay Hospital, Nambour Hospital, Toowoomba Hospital, Mt Isa Hospital and Bundaberg Hospital.

Primary Injury Services: These services are available in most other hospitals including rural and urban areas. Queensland Ambulance Service transports most trauma patients to the hospitals where trauma services are available.

Primary Health Services: This service is to provide aid in emergencies to injured patients.

Private Health Facilities: Private hospitals can be categorised according to Clinical Service Capability.

The Queensland Ambulance Service (QAS): QAS is run by Queensland government's Department of Community Safety and is the fourth-largest ambulance service in the world. This service provides services with the public by more than 260 ambulance locations across the state. Their services include emergency response, pre-hospital patient cares, specialised transport services, coordinated aero-medical services and inter-hospital transfers. Advanced Care Paramedics (ACPs) are competent in emergency medical skills, including airway management, cardiac management (ECG, defibrillation), drug/fluid administration and the administration of basic and some levels of advanced drugs (Queensland Ambulance 2008).

The Royal Flying Doctor Service (RFDS): RFDS established in 1928, is a non-profit organisation. It is delivering health services to the people who are living, working or travelling in rural, remote and coastal Queensland. RFDS has total eight bases in Brisbane, Bundaberg, Cairns, Charleville, Longreach, Mount Isa, Rockhampton and Townsville (Royal Flying Doctor 2016).

3.2.2 Simulated Case Studies

A simulated case study (this is a simulated case based on scenario developed out of real life experience) is considered where a motor vehicle accident occurred on Bruce Highway near Mount Larcom, Central Queensland and Australia. It is a hot day in December. A family of four (husband, wife and two kids, eight and one-year-old boy and girl) was coming from Brisbane to Rockhampton to spend Christmas with parents and family. They started at 7 am in the morning and had two breaks on the way. The husband was driving and he was very tired. It was around 2 pm and the outside temperature was close to 40 °C. A semitrailer, which was coming from the opposite side was trying to overtake a campervan and had head-on collision with the car. The car fell into a ditch. The boy managed to get out of the car but other passengers were seriously injured and the driver was unconscious. The semitrailer did not stop. The boy managed to take out his dad's mobile phone from his pocket and called the emergency number. Ambulance and fire service arrived 22 min later. After a couple of checks and discussion with the Clinical Supervisor, paramedic decided to take the driver to nearest MRTS (Rockhampton hospital) by helicopter and rest of the family to nearest Gladstone Base Hospital by ambulance. The driver had major injury. When Rockhampton hospital assessed his situation as critical, they decided to transfer him to RBWH. When they reached RBWH, there were patients waiting for OT. Further communication revealed diversion to nearest MTS (Gold Coast hospital) by helicopter. Delays in diversion had its toll. The patient passed away on the way to Gold Coast. Similar to this case study, suboptimal diversion can result in the increased mortality and morbidity rate to 82% compared to 30% if appropriate surgical cares can be initiated within 4 h of injury (Rogers et al. 1999; Danne et al. 1998). In this case, it took one hour from the point of first call to organise the helicopter and pilot to pick up and drop the patient to Rockhampton hospital. When Rockhampton hospital assessed the case as critical, they analysed the availability of resources such as OT and bed, neurosurgeon, pathology and radiology facilities in MTS and decided transfer to RBWH. By the time helicopter arrived RBWH, OT was having patients at a level above their full capacity. Nearest hospital PAH whose helipad was under renovation and radiology was temporarily out of service. Gold Coast hospital was only one diversion option for the definitive care. The whole process took six hours from the time of first call to patient admission to hospital. On the basis of the existing health care structure the following model is created.

3.2.3 Model

Within this proposed model, there are two sub-models for analysing the impact of resources on the performances of trauma services based on waiting time, delays and diversions for reducing the time to reach the definite care from the point of first call.

3.2.3.1 MRTS or MTS

In this illustrative case, two sub-models are—(i) MRTS of Rockhampton hospital and (ii) MTS of RBWS and PAH in Brisbane. Each sub-model comprises five blocks—(i) accident scene, (ii) regional QAS station, (iii) despatch of vehicle, (iv) accident spot with paramedic care and (iv) LH. In this process model transports including ambulance, helicopter and jet plane are used for patient transfer from accident spot to appropriate hospital.

Decision at the Accident Scene

There are six severity levels and this module incorporates first point of call after accident time and decides the action according to the severity level of trauma. The decision-making process is described as follows:

(i) Severity 1—Go home from scene
(ii) Severity 2—Go to LH by ambulance
(iii) Severity 3—Go to MRTS by ambulance
(iv) Severity 4—Go to MRTS by helicopter
(v) Severity 5—Go to MTS by helicopter and jet plane
(vi) Severity 6—Go to MTS by RFDS.

Decision of Transport Mode

Depending on the severity of trauma, distance to the appropriate trauma care facility and availability of one of the transports—ambulance, helicopter and RFDS, decisions are taken to transport a patient using the following general rules used for transportation:

- LH (local hospital) by ambulance or helicopter
- MRTS by ambulance or helicopter or,
- MTS by jet plane from MRTS
- Regional QAS station is responsible for ambulance movement.

It is a common rule that for transferring a patient from scene to the LH, only ambulance is used.

3.2.3.2 The Main Resources Decision Model

The main resources decision model contains helipad station and helicopter activity, RFDS station and jet plane activity, two local hospitals' sub-model connectivity, calendar, MRTS and MTS. They are described as follows:

- Helipad and RFDS stations are responsible for the transport by helicopter, jet plane and Royal Flying doctors.
- Statistics of the accident rates are different in QLD during holidays, wet condition of the road and night time. Calendar provides the probabilistic accident rates.
- In case of seriously injured patient, the patient is transported to MRTS or MTS by helicopter or jet plane.
- MTS is normally in RBWS and PAH, Brisbane, QLD, Australia.

Integrated model

Integrated model (see Fig. 3.1) proposed here is developed by using Rockwell software Arena (https://www.arenasimulation.com/) to analyse the effectiveness of trauma management system. Figure 3.1 shows local hospitals, MRTS, MTS, accident spots, network connectivity and relevant processes.

Real life data were collected from the Queensland Health for inter process time stamps and estimating the parameters of the underlying relations and distributions. Three sets of sample of these data are shown in the Tables 3.1, 3.2 and 3.3.

The locations of five local hospitals (shown in 1–5), one MRTS (6) and two MTS (7 and 8) are presented as follows:

1. Gladstone Hospital, Gladstone 4680
2. Biloela Hospital, Biloela 4712
3. Emerald Hospital, Emerald 4720
4. Springsure Hospital, Springsure 4722
5. Yeppoon Hospital, Yeppoon 4703
6. MRTS in Rockhampton Hospital, Rockhampton 4701
7. MTS in Royal Brisbane and Women's Hospital, Brisbane 4029
8. MTS in PA Hospital, Brisbane 4102.

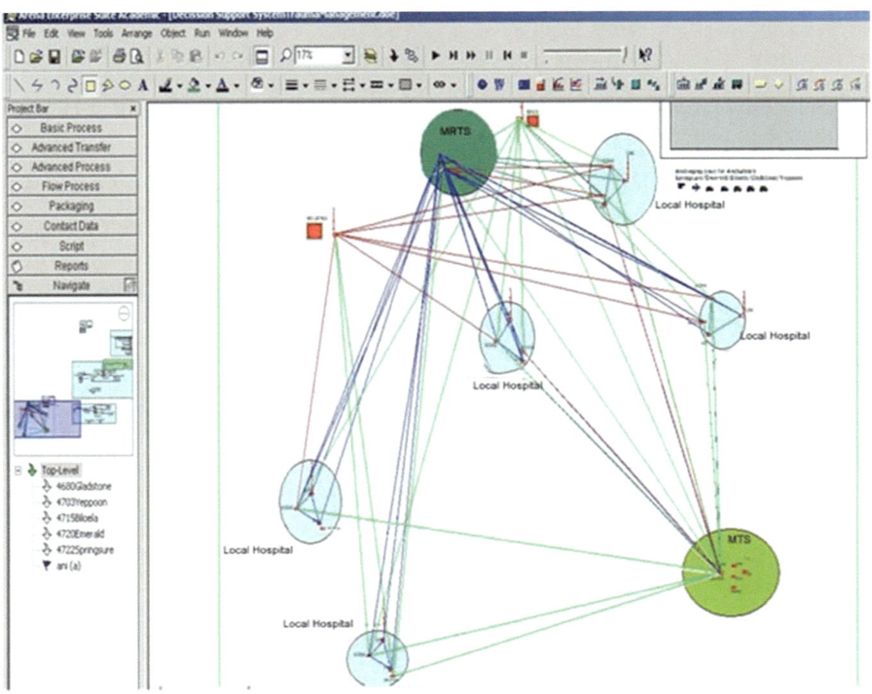

Fig. 3.1 Integrated model using Rockwell software Arena

Table 3.1 Pre-hospital sample data

Item #	Description	Time start	Actual time	Date	Mode of arrival
1	Request	19:42		XXXXXX	Helicopter
2	Dispatch	19:42			
3	Scene arrival	20:28			
4	Scene Departure	21:36			
5	First hospital arrival	22:03			
6	First observation	21:22			
7	Scene time		00:38		
8	Pre-hospital time		02:18		

Table 3.2 Local hospital sample data

Item #	Description	Time start	Actual time	Date	Mode of arrival
1	Local hospital arrival	22:10			Ambulance
2	Local hospital departure	11:42		Next day	
3	Transferred patient to MTS				
4	Time delay—transferred patient to MTS		13:32		

3.3 Simulation

Simulation model was constructed considering the above mentioned scenarios and ran for one-year period with alternate resource parameters using Arena simulation software. This analysis shows how the resource constraints impact the performance of trauma management services. The analysis of having MRI (in care facility, not considered in current analysis and can be considered in future work) and additional helicopters in remote places in the critical time of trauma patients and reduction of number of diversions and total time between first point of call and definitive care is the expected benefits of the model.

For each scenario, the waiting time required a patient having an accident at the place with postcode 4680 to reach a definitive care produced by the simulation model with 30 replications are shown in Table 3.4.

The waiting time of a patient to reach a definite care depends on the number of emergency calls received, and services and resources availability around the time of first point of call. Our aim is to predict the maximum waiting time for the duration of the simulation time for each scenario. Since the maximum waiting time distribution closely reflects the Gumbel distribution, a special case of extreme value distribution (https://en.wikipedia.org/wiki/Gumbel_distribution), the Gumbel distribution is used in the simulation to estimate the waiting time.

Table 3.3 MTS sample data

Item #	Description	Time start	Actual time	Date	Mode of arrival
1	Emergency department			Next	Fixed
	Admission	14:31		Day	Wing
ED bypassed to OT					
2	Definitive care				
3	Trauma service				
	Admission	xx:xx			
	Discharge	08:13		10th day	
4	ICU				
	Admission	14:42			
	Discharge	12:10		17th day	
Duration: 12 days 0.28					
5	Acute Care				
	Admission	14:31			
	Discharge	12:10		17th day	
Duration: 12 days 0.39					
6	Rehabilitation				
	Admission	12:10		17th day	
	Discharge	12:00		xxxxxx	
Duration: 204 days					
Total					
	Admission	14:31		xxxxxx	
	Discharge	12:00		xxxxxx	
	Duration: 219 days	Outcome: Survived			

Table 3.4 The waiting time analysis at the accident scene having postcode 4680 for Scenarios 1, 2 and 3

Item #	Ambulance	Helicopter	Jet plane	Min	Average	Max
A. Scenario 1						
1	2			0.190	0.245	0.598
2		1		0.570	0.767	2.298
3			1	0.422	0.607	6.370
B. Scenario 2						
1	5			0.073	0.098	0.167
2		2		0.274	0.412	1.864
3			2	0.204	0.262	0.315
C. Scenario 3						
1	8			0.0454	0.061	0.074
2		4		0.141	0.164	0.200
3			4	0.108	0.139	0.1605

Table 3.5 The improvement of waiting time with additional resources compare to Scenario 1

Item #	Ambulance waiting Time	Improvement (%)	Helicopter waiting time	Improvement (%)	Jet plane waiting time	Improvement (%)
Sc-1	0.598		2.298		6.370	
Sc-2	0.167	72	1.864	18	0.315	95
Sc-3	0.081	86	0.200	91	0.1605	97

Substantial improvement of waiting time occurs with the increase of available ambulances as waiting times are 0.59, 0.26 and 0.081 when two, four and six ambulances are available, respectively.

The improvements of waiting time for Scenarios 2 and 3 compared with Scenario 1 are shown in Table 3.5.

Table 3.5 shows that the improvements of waiting time for Scenarios 2 and 3 are 72 and 86% for ambulance, respectively, while they are 18 and 91%, and 95 and 97% for helicopter and jet planes. Investment through strategic planning to cope with the dynamic requests from traumatic patients will certainly reduce the waiting time significantly to transfer patients to a definitive care and save life.

3.4 Conclusion

Managing trauma is a challenge for regional Queensland where natural disasters are occurring more frequently, distances are huge and resources are constrained. This research defines a framework for developing an efficient integrated trauma management system for analysing the impact of resources on performance. ITMS with DSS capability is proposed to be linked to QAS monitor, clinical supervisor's network and resources in LH, MTS and MRTS hospitals. It is expected to provide faster and better decision-making that will reduce delays and help faster and appropriate treatment if extended to tactical and operational planning. This will help deciding on adequate resources, appropriate diversions and transfers. Proposed system is expected to improve patient outcome by reducing mortality and morbidity significantly and provide better health care services to people living in remote places in regional Queensland.

References

About Australia. *Queensland Map*. http://www.about-australia.com/maps/queensland. Accessed 16 Sept 2016.

American College of Surgeons, Advanced trauma life support. https://www.facs.org/quality-programs/trauma/atls. Accessed 7 Sept 2016.

Australian Bureau of Statistics. http://www.abs.gov.au. Accessed 7 Sept 2016.

Australian Government. *Geoscience Australia: State and Territory Borders*. http://www.ga.gov.au . Accessed 16 Sept 2016.

Butler, T. W., Karwan, K. R., & Sweigart, J. R. (1992). Multi-level strategic evaluations of hospital plans and decisions. *Journal of the Operation Research Society, 43,* 662–672.

Chen, C. Y., Chen, P. Y., & Chen, W. T. (2013). A novel emergency vehicle dispatching system. In *IEEE 77th vehicular technology conference*. Dresden, Germany: VTC Spring.

Daskin, M.S., & Dean, L.K. (2004). Location of health care facilities. In Brandeau, M.L., Sainfort, F., Pierskalla, W.P. (Eds.), *Operations Research and Health Care*. A Handbook of Methods and Applications. Kluwer's International Series, Dordrecht, pp. 43–76.

Danne, P., et al. (1998). The major trauma management study: an analysis of the efficacy of current trauma care. *ANZ Journal of Surgery, 68*(1), 20–27.

FitzGerald, G., et al. (2006). A trauma plan for Queensland. http://citeseerx.ist.psu.edu/viewdoc/download?doi=10.1.1.134.6053andrep=rep1andtype=pdf. Accessed 8 Sept 2016.

Fitzgerald, G., Tippett, V., Schuetz, M., & Pollard, C. (2008). The Queensland trauma plan project. *ANZ Journal of Surgery, 78*(9), 780–783.

Lei, C., Lin, W. H., & Miao, L. (2015). A stochastic emergency vehicle redeployment model for an effective response to traffic incidents. *IEEE Transactions on Intelligent Transportation Systems, 16*(2), 898–909.

Meadows, G., Ozmen, M., Patten, S., Brooker, J., Shawyer, F., Kamruzzaman, J., et al. (2013). Estimating the long term effects on depression prevalence of introducing Mindfulness Based Cognitive Therapy to target depressive relapse; a simulation modelling approach. In *14th International Congress of the IFPE 'The uses of psychiatric epidemiology in improving population mental health'*, Leipzig, Germany.

Queensland Ambulance. *Queensland Ambulance Service Divisional Plan 2008–2012*. http://www.ambulance.qld.gov.au. Accessed 16 Sept 2016.

Rogers, F. B., Shackford, S. R., Osler, T. M., Vane, D. W., & Davis, J. H. (1999). Rural trauma: the challenge for the next decade. *Journal of Trauma, 47*(4), 802–811.

Royal Australian College of Surgeons, Trauma committee and sub-committees. http://www.surgeons.org/member-services/interest-groups-sections/trauma/trauma-committee-and-sub-committees/. Accessed 7 Sept 2016.

Royal Flying Doctor. *Media Materials*. http://www.flyingdoctor.org.au. Accessed 16 Sept 2016.

Thi Nguyen, N. H. (2015). *Quantitative analysis of ambulance location-allocation and ambulance state prediction*. Department of Science and Technology, Linköping University, Norrköping, Sweden.

Worthington, D. J. (1987). Queuing models for hospital waiting lists. *Journal of Operation Research Society, 38,* 413–422.

Worthington, D. (1991). Hospital waiting lists models. *The Journal of the Operational Research Society, 42*(10), 833–843.

Yang, D., Liu, M., & Su, Q. (2016). Cost-effective analyses of joint planning in emergency medical services: a case study. In *13th International Conference on Service Systems and Service Management (ICSSSM)*, Kunming, China.

Chapter 4
Regulatory Mechanism for Diagnostic Radiology (DR) Facilities in India

Anirban Guin, Soujanya Mukherjee, Manas Kumar Pathak and A.U. Sonawane

Abstract Radiology is one kind of diagnostic imaging technology for early diagnosis and prevention of disease that employs X-ray ionizing radiation for imaging of anatomical structure inside the body. The X-ray beam passing through the body gets attenuated by a varying degree depending upon the bone density, soft tissue content, muscle, water content, etc., inside the body and the transmitted X-ray beam is used to form an image of anatomical structure inside the body. At present, around 90,000 X-ray machines are in operation in India. In order to ensure safety of personnel involved in operation of different types of diagnostic radiology equipment as well as safety of the members of public, Atomic Energy Regulatory Board (AERB) exercises the powers conferred by the Atomic Energy Act, 1962 in India. The Mission of AERB is to ensure that safe use of ionizing radiation and nuclear energy in India does not cause any undue risk to the health of people and the environment. AERB issues different types of consents like registration, license for operation of diagnostic radiology facility. Before issue of consent, detailed reviews are carried out, and consent is issued for a specific period of time. Regular, special or surprise inspections are also carried out for verification of radiological safety status in diagnostic radiology facilities. Chairman, AERB, is the competent authority under the Atomic Energy (Radiation Protection) Rules, 2004 and issues time to time directives and notifications prescribing dose limits, radiation warning symbol, etc. AERB publishes several safety related documents like codes, guides, and standards for effective regulation of stakeholders like manufacturers, suppliers, service agencies, and users of diagnostic radiology equipment in the country. It is mandatory to obtain license/registration from AERB for operation of diagnostic radiology equipment. In order to strengthen and streamline the process, AERB has launched a web-based application named e-Licensing of Radiation Applications (e-LORA) for automation of regulatory process. With the increasing number of diagnostic radiology facilities in today's scenario, effective regulatory control is a

A. Guin · S. Mukherjee · M.K. Pathak (✉)
Atomic Energy Regulatory Board, Eastern Regional Regulatory Centre, Kolkata, India
e-mail: mkpathak@vecc.gov.in

A.U. Sonawane
Radiological Safety Division, Atomic Energy Regulatory Board, Mumbai, India

P.K. Ray and J. Maiti (eds.), *Healthcare Systems Management: Methodologies and Applications*, Managing the Asian Century,
DOI 10.1007/978-981-10-5631-4_4

challenging task. This paper brings out different modalities of effective and efficient regulation of diagnostic radiology facilities of the country, detailing on the varied experiences acquired in the process, as well as preparedness of the regulatory body in meeting up with the challenges in future.

Keywords Ionizing radiation · Consent · Shielding · PMS · QA

4.1 Introduction

Medical X-rays using ionizing radiation has become an essential tool for protecting and improving human health since its discovery at the end of nineteenth century. In X-ray diagnostics, radiation that is partly transmitted through and partly absorbed in the irradiated object is utilized to show the variations in transmission caused by structures in the object of varying thickness, density, or atomic composition. Thus, when X-ray passes through a human body, it gets attenuated by a varying degree depending upon the bone density, soft tissue content, muscle, water content, etc., inside the body, and the transmitted X-ray beam is used to form an image of the anatomical structure of the human body. Commonly used diagnostic radiology using ionizing radiation are plain radiography, computed tomography (CT), interventional radiology (Cath Lab), Bone Mineral Densitometry (BMD), Orthopantomography (OPG), etc.

Maximum dose received by a typical patient undergoing X-ray procedure ranges within ~ 0.7 mSv for plain radiography, ~ 10 mSv for CT scan, and 7.5–57.0 mSv for interventional procedures. Over 90% of the workload in diagnostic radiology in many countries is the general radiography and is a major contributor to the collective population dose. In India, at present, around 90,000 X-ray machines are in operation throughout the country. As unsafe use of X-ray radiation has health risks associated with it, proper care is required to be exercised throughout the life cycle of the equipment, viz. manufacture, supply, installation, use, maintenance, service and ultimately, decommissioning. It is therefore essential, from the radiological safety view point, to exercise strict regulatory control over the safe use of such beneficial application of ionizing radiation.

4.2 Regulatory Framework

In the international platform, organizations/agencies like International Atomic Energy Agency (IAEA), International Commission on Radiological Protection (ICRP), National Council on Radiation Protection (NCRP), USA, National Radiological Protection Board (NRPB), UK, etc., provide guidelines pertaining to safe applications of radiation for different applications. In India, the regulatory framework for controlling safe use of ionizing radiation, including medical X-rays, is mainly based on the Atomic Energy Act, 1962 and the Atomic Energy Radiation Protection Rules, 2004.

The national regulatory authority, i.e., Atomic Energy Regulatory Board (AERB) was constituted on November 15, 1983 by the President of India to exercise the regulatory and safety functions envisaged under Sections 16, 17, and 23 of the Atomic Energy Act (1962). Chairman, AERB has been notified as the Competent Authority for the enforcement of radiation protection in the country. The mission of the board is to ensure that the use of ionizing radiation and nuclear energy in India does not cause undue risk to the health of people and the environment.

The Atomic Energy (Radiation Protection) Rules [AE (RP) R] (1971) promulgated under the Atomic Energy Act (1962), provides the legal framework for the safe handling of radiation generating equipment. It is mandatory for all the manufacturers, suppliers, and users to obtain requisite license from AERB for carrying out any activity related to ionizing radiation (Atomic Energy Radiation Protection Rules 1971). The minimum safety-related requirements/obligations to be met by a nuclear or radiation facility to qualify for issue of regulatory consent at every stage leading to eventual operation is spelt out in the Safety Code on Regulation of Nuclear and Radiation Facilities (No. AERB/SC/G 2000).

For effective implementation of regulations in the country, AERB has established its Regional Regulatory Centers (RRC) at Chennai, Kolkata, and Delhi, respectively for regulation of southern, eastern, and northern regions of the country in addition to its headquarters at Mumbai.

Considering the large number of widespread X-ray facilities, AERB has initiated steps for formation of Directorate of Radiation Safety (DRS)[1] under Health and Family Welfare Department of every state, to carry out regulatory inspections of X-ray facilities (of the state) and support the utilities in obtaining license from AERB.

4.3 Graded Approach in Regulation

For DR facilities, two types of regulatory consents, viz. 'License' and 'Registration', are applicable and this is based on the radiological hazard potential of the concerned facility. AERB follows a graded approach towards regulation of different radiation facilities within its purview.

'Graded Approach' is "An application of safety requirements that is commensurate with the characteristics of the facilities and activities or the source and with

[1]Memorandum of Understanding between AERB and Department of Health and Family Welfare, covering the terms and conditions agreed upon to participate in regulatory inspections of DR facilities.

the magnitude and likelihood of the exposures". Para 3.15 of Fundamental Safety Principles (IAEA Safety Fundamentals 2006) states, "Safety has to be assessed and periodically reassessed throughout the lifetime of facilities and activities, consistent with a graded approach." [AE (RP) R] (1971) broadly classifies the licenses for operation of radiation facilities as License, Authorization, and Registration, based on the associated hazard potential, with an intent to follow the graded approach of regulation.

AERBs Safety Guide on "Consenting Process for Radiation Facilities" (No. AERB/RF/SG/G-3 Vols. 1–4 2011) specifies detailed requirements for issue of consents for radiation facilities from the standpoint of safe operation and protection of the operating personnel, the general public and the environment from radiological hazards.

The hazard potential of a given type of facility is determined by the relative chances of inadvertent exposures to patients, workers or the general public (in normal or abnormal scenarios). Based on this requirement, the consenting process for diagnostic radiology is graded into license and registration with license being for higher hazard potential like CT and Cath Lab while registration is for lower hazard potential like fixed X-ray, OPG etc.

4.4 e-Licensing of Radiation Applications (e-LORA)

It is mandatory for all the manufacturers, suppliers, and users of DR equipment to obtain requisite license from AERB. In view of this, to facilitate online submission of applications for different regulatory consents, AERB has launched a web-based application for smooth and effective end-to-end regulatory processes through e-LORA. Implementation of e-LORA system has helped in management of national inventory and monitoring movement of radiation generating equipment; management of regulatory inspections, non-compliances and enforcement directives; management of radiation professional, RSO and radiation worker; automation in workflow and review of submissions for quick processing of applications.

Before the advent of the e-LORA system, only about 5000 X-ray equipments were licensed with AERB, through offline 'hard-copy' processing. However, the implementation of e-LORA system has witnessed unprecedented response from several utilities. In a period of less than 2 years, more than 28,000 X-ray equipments have been brought under the ambit of regulation of AERB with the help of e-LORA. The main features of the online system that proved to be the hallmark of effective and efficient regulation includes quick review and processing of applications, provision of full reliability and transparency in dealing of applications, showing real-time processing status to utility, and preservation of all related documents for future reference, if required.

4.5 Radiation Safety in DR Facilities

Total radiation safety in DR practices is achieved by 'Built-in' safety, combined with 'Operational' safety. The Safety Code on 'Medical Diagnostic X-ray Equipment and Installations' (No. AERB/RF-MED/SC-3 (Rev.2) 2015), published by AERB is intended to govern total radiation safety in design, installation, and operation of X-ray equipment for medical diagnostic purposes. Implementation of provisions of the Safety Code ensures adequate radiation protection for occupational workers, patients, and the general public at large. In line with the motto to protect people and environment from undue risk due to use of ionizing radiation, AERB has formulated a list of precautionary measures so as to prevent inadvertent exposures of occupational workers, patients, and general public from ionizing radiation in DR facilities.

4.5.1 Built-in Safety

AERB ensures that sufficient protection against the harmful effects of radiation is built-into the facility handling diagnostic X-ray equipment by allowing the use of only 'type-approved' X-ray machines, and approving only those facilities where the construction of the X-ray room installation and its accessories are as per the guidelines prescribed by AERB.

4.5.1.1 Type Approval

The 'type approval' process of X-ray equipment involves subjecting it to a series of test conditions with stringent qualifying requirements to ensure conformance to adequate radiation safety standards and design requirements. Only those X-ray units need to be procured by the users which have been 'type approved' (AERB Safety Code 2015). It is thus mandatory that only valid 'type approved' diagnostic X-ray equipment are marketed and used in the country. In order to implement this, AERB issues 'No Objection (NOC)' certificates for importing X-ray equipment of a new make/model from a foreign country, or 'type approval' certificates for procuring from indigenous manufacturers, after it is ensured that the machine meets all the safety criteria as required by the type approval process.

Some of the design requirements that need to be met by the X-ray diagnostic equipment for type approval include maximum radiation leakage from the tube housing within prescribed limits, alignment of radiation, and light field within tolerance limits, minimum total filtration of X-ray tube for maximum rated operating tube potential, and accuracy of Automatic Exposure Control (AEC) system.

4.5.1.2 Layout and Shielding

X-ray equipment must be installed in adequately shielded rooms to ensure that public in the vicinity of the X-ray installations are not unduly exposed to X-ray radiation. The adequacy of shielding depends on the material and thickness used for this purpose. Different materials can be used for shielding. However, brick or concrete are considered the best materials, as they are easily available, economical, and have good structural strength. AERB has made available detailed layout and shielding guidelines applicable for different types of DR facilities in India at its official website for ready reference (2016). These are at par or even better than the international requirements. Some of the parameters that are taken into account while carrying out shielding calculations of a DR facility include design dose/week, use factor, occupancy factor and workload (NCRP 2004). It has been made mandatory to take approval with regard to adequacy of layout and shielding for CT and Cath Lab before procurement. The final assessment of the adequacy of the design and structural shielding is based on the radiation survey of the installation at the time of commissioning of the equipment.

4.5.2 Operational Safety

'Operational' safety is ensured before according license for regular operation of the facility. During this process, it is checked that qualified manpower is available to operate the facility, adequate personnel dose monitoring service exists, all necessary personnel protective accessories are kept in sufficient numbers, and that proper mechanism is available to ensure periodic servicing/maintenance and Quality Assurance (QA) checks of the X-ray equipment as per regulatory requirements.

4.5.2.1 Manpower Requirements

Based on the hazard potential, X-ray installations need to have radiologist, related medical practitioner and technician with adequate knowledge to operate the X-ray equipment (AERB 2012). Each and every DR facility needs to have one person designated as Radiological Safety Officer (RSO), who will be responsible for advising and assisting the facility owner on radiation safety aspects.

4.5.2.2 Personnel Monitoring Service (PMS)

One of the key principles of radiation protection is called 'Optimization', which is essentially related to the dose uptake by a typical radiation worker during the course of his work. It means that any work involving radiation should be planned meticulously in such a manner, that the workers involved are exposed 'As Low As

Reasonably Achievable (ALARA)'. Thus the collective dose of the team involved in the radiation-related job is 'optimized' in order to achieve ALARA.

It is necessary to monitor and control the dose received by the radiation workers during the work. It is the responsibility of the licensee of the DR facility to ensure that the radiation workers of the facility comply with the dose limits and regulatory constraints as specified by the competent authority (Atomic Energy Radiation Protection Rules 1971). Chairman, AERB being the Competent Authority has issued safety directive (no. 11/2011) (AERB 2011) prescribing the dose limits for exposures from ionizing radiations for workers and the members of the public, which needs to be adhered to.

In addition to dose limits, AERB has prescribed certain regulatory constraints, which are much lower than the dose limits. A DR facility should try to optimize the work so that none of the radiation worker is exposed beyond the regulatory constraints. In case these are exceeded, AERB is intimated regarding the same, and a detailed investigation process to that effect is initiated. A separate committee in this regard has been constituted by AERB to take up such 'excessive exposure' cases to carry out investigation and accordingly recommend suitable corrective actions so as to prevent similar recurrences in future.

In order to adhere to the aforementioned dose limits and regulatory constraints, the radiation personnel of the facility needs to be provided with suitable 'monitoring' mechanisms for the dose received. This is called 'Personnel Monitoring Service (PMS)'. It involves a systematic process for monitoring, recording, evaluating, and reporting of radiation doses received by occupationally exposed individuals. Availability of PMS for all the radiation workers (including trainees) of DR facility has been made mandatory in order to obtain license (AERB Safety Code 2015).

The monitoring of individual doses received by radiation workers is carried out by special devices called 'dosimeters'. The most common type of dosimeters in vogue today is the 'Thermo-Luminescent Dosimeter (TLD)'. It is necessary for all the radiation workers to 'wear' these dosimeters provided to them, while carrying out radiation-related work. The occupational doses received by the personnel is recorded and 'stored' in the device. However, in order to know the actual dose received, the device has to be 'read' by following special scientific techniques. This evaluation process is carried out by specialized laboratories in the country, which have been identified region-wise. The TLD badges of all the radiation workers of a particular DR facility are sent to these laboratories (region-wise) after every quarter, for the doses to be evaluated and accordingly recorded and reported back to the facility. National occupational Dose Registry (NODRS) system maintains the dose record of the radiation worker in India.

4.5.2.3 Personnel Protective Accessories

Suitable protective devices like mobile protective barrier, protective aprons, gloves, thyroid and gonad shields, and protective goggles need to be used during operation of a diagnostic radiology unit in order to minimize dose uptake.

It is evident that in order to effectively protect the occupational worker from radiation, use of personnel protective devices should always be ensured. Further, these devices need to be periodically verified for their shielding adequacy, and in case of any noticeable degradation, should be replaced with new ones.

4.5.2.4 Surveillance and QA Checks

One of the fundamental goals in diagnostic radiology is to provide the best possible image quality with minimum radiation dose and at minimum cost to the patient and institution. To achieve this, it is essential that a quality assurance (QA) and surveillance programme be developed and implemented in X-ray diagnostic departments. If the image is of poor quality, radiologists may not be able to extract diagnostic information from the radiograph, which may necessitate repetition of patient examination (retake). Retakes result in unnecessary radiation dose to patients, workers, and public. Retakes also result in overloading of the machine that reduces the tube life. The QA programme in DR facilities aim at obtaining good-quality images with optimal doses, which would considerably reduce the chances of retakes and thereby patient dose.

The QA programme begins with the performance evaluation tests of the X-ray diagnostic equipment at the manufacturing stage and then the acceptance tests after the installation of the units for users to ensure conformity with the specifications. The QA tests are carried out thereafter at regular intervals and also after major repairs that might affect the performance of equipment or when equipment malfunction is suspected. The QA test process involves carrying out QA tests as per approved procedures laid out by AERB, recording of results, analyzing the equipment performance, and carry out repeat tests after taking suitable corrective measures if the previous performance analysis was not satisfactory.

Periodic QA checks of diagnostic equipment in possession of DR facilities is also mandated in AERB Safety Code (2015). In order to carry out the tests, facility owners must avail the services of AERB authorized service agencies. AERB has laid down detailed authorization procedure for service agencies in this regard, and a list of such agencies is also available at the official website.

In QA tests, the accuracy and consistency of a number of parameters, which influence the quality of diagnostic image and patient dose, are checked. These include congruence of optical and radiation fields, central beam alignment, focal spot size, exposure time, applied tube potential, total filtration, linearity of timer/mA loading stations, consistence of radiation output, and radiation leakage through tube housing.

The tools required for each of the above tests, the desired frequency, as well as the acceptance criteria is mentioned in detail in the QA procedures and guidelines framed by AERB (format is available at AERB website) (2016).

4.6 License/Registration

Once a DR facility has been able to demonstrate the adequacy with respect to 'built-in', as well as 'operational' safety requirements, the license/registration is issued for operation of the facility for a given time period. Tools like regulatory inspection and enforcement,[2] review of periodic safety status report, review of unusual occurrence, etc., are used to ensure adequate regulatory oversight throughout the operating period of the DR facility.

After the expiry of the license, the facility needs to reapply for renewal of license. In case the facility decides to decommission the unit, the same should be carried out by authorized agencies with prior intimation to the Competent Authority.

4.7 Public Awareness

AERB organizes various kinds of public awareness programmes throughout the country in the form of trainings, exhibitions, seminars, etc. These programmes aims to disseminate necessary information with regard to various regulatory requirements relevant to radiological safety in radiation facilities as well as sensitize the facility owners, occupational workers and general public with respect to safe and secure use of ionizing radiation.

4.8 Conclusion

Although the medical uses of X-rays to examine a patient has proved to be an amazing medical diagnostic tool, X-rays have negative side effects due to its use of radiation in the process. During X-ray examination, not only the patient gets exposed to radiation but also the persons around the X-ray equipment, albeit to a lower extent.

AERB has the responsibility to promote the safe use of the equipment in order to minimize radiation hazard to patient, operator and members of public. One of the ways to ensure radiation safety is to create awareness among everyone concerned. It is the responsibility of the owners of the DR facilities to ensure that the radiation workers are aware of the harmful effects of radiation and accordingly, take adequate safety measures. In this regard, a DR facility operating with a valid license from AERB, and obeying all the safety precautions as prescribed, may be considered safe as far as radiological hazards are concerned.

---

[2]AERB Safety Manual on "Regulatory Inspection and Enforcement in Radiation Facilities" (No. AERB/RF/SM/G-3).

References

AERB Directive No. 01/2011 vide ref no. CH/AERB/ITSD/125/2011/1507 dated April 27, 2011.

AERB notification on "Prescribed qualifications and experience for personnel in medical X-ray installations", vide ref no. AERB/RSD/MDX/Sp-order/2012/14316 dated November 26, 2012.

AERB Safety Code on "Regulation of Nuclear and Radiation Facilities" (No. AERB/SC/G) dated August, 2000.

AERB Safety Code on "Radiation Safety in Manufacture, Supply and Use of Medical Diagnostic X-ray Equipment", No. AERB/RF-MED/SC-3 (Rev.2), 2015.

AERB Safety Guide on "Consenting Process for Radiation Facilities" (No. AERB/RF/SG/G-3 Vols. 1–4), March, 2011.

Atomic Energy Act, No. 33, issued September 15, 1962, amended no. 59 dated December 23, 1986 and vide no. 29 dated September 8, 1987.

Atomic Energy Radiation Protection Rules 1971, amended on September 11, 2004 (GSR 303).

IAEA Safety Fundamentals (IAEA Safety Standards Series No. SF-1), 2006.

NCRP report no. 147 on "Structural Shielding Design for Medical X-Ray Imaging Facilities" (2004).

Sample layout plans and QA formats available at Atomic Energy Regulatory Board official website http://www.aerb.gov.in/AERBPortal/pages/English/X-Ray/X-Ray.jsp. Accessed October 5, 2016.

Chapter 5
Healthcare Improvement Through Integration of Quality Initiatives

Sujata Mitra, Sudhir Mishra and Pankaj Kumar

Abstract Tata Main Hospital (TMH), Jamshedpur is a 920-bedded hospital of Tata Steel providing free health care to employees and their families. It is a referral centre for others who pay for services. In the past 20 years, the hospital has moved from unstructured, random quality improvement projects to implementing international and national quality standards like ISO and NABH. As part of Tata Steel, the hospital introduced QIP and VE projects in 1992. In 1995, the JN Tata Excellence Model was rolled out. The hospital was certified to ISO 9001: 2008 in 2010. Subsequently, it adopted policy and daily management with formulation of ABP (Annual Business Plan) and cascaded these as departmental KPIs (key performance indicator). NABH standards were implemented in National Accreditation Board for Hospital and Healthcare Providers (NABH) (Accreditation standards for hospitals (3rd ed) 2011). The ISO and NABH standards were integrated with the daily management and healthcare protocols were developed. These were implemented in all work areas, administrative and clinical. To provide a strong base to the integrated system, document control was on LAN. Monitoring was through structured internal audits and a formal review mechanism. TMH achieved ISO certification in 2010 and recertification in 2016. NABH pre-accreditation certification was obtained in April 2016. A total of 42 quality parameters are reviewed through the integrated system and many of these have shown significant improvement over the years (morbidity, wait time, and satisfaction-related data). Through an integrated approach to quality, Tata Main Hospital helped to set up an improvement cycle with focus on patient satisfaction, quality of health care and cost. Improvement has been recorded on all three perspectives.

S. Mitra (✉)
Department of Nuclear Medicine, Tata Main Hospital, Jamshedpur 831001, India
e-mail: sujatamitra@tatasteel.com

S. Mishra
Department of Paediatrics, Tata Main Hospital, Jamshedpur 831001, India
e-mail: drsudhir@tatasteel.com

P. Kumar
Human Resource Management, Tata Steel, Jamshedpur 831001, India
e-mail: pankajkumar@tatasteel.com

P.K. Ray and J. Maiti (eds.), *Healthcare Systems Management: Methodologies and Applications*, Managing the Asian Century,
DOI 10.1007/978-981-10-5631-4_5

Keywords Health care · Quality · Integrated standards

5.1 Introduction

Tata Main Hospital (TMH), Jamshedpur is a 920-bedded multi-specialty hospital providing curative health care through outpatient, inpatient (including critical care), and emergency services. As part of Tata Steel, the hospital introduced basic quality tools like quality improvement and value engineering projects in 1992. However, these were stand-alone initiatives involving specific work areas and did not impact the quality of health care significantly. In an effort to bring in sustained improvement involving the entire hospital, the JN Tata Excellence Model, based on the Malcolm Baldridge criteria (Health Care Criteria for Performance Excellence, Baldridge National Quality Program 2001), was adopted in 1999 which resulted in development of healthcare-specific balance score card, customer focus, and monitoring of financial and patient satisfaction-related parameters (Mitra 2001a, b). However, the anticipated improvement in the core area of patient care was not evident. TMH was certified to ISO 9001: 2008 in 2010. Subsequently, the hospital set itself the goal to achieve NABH (National Accreditation Board for Hospitals and Healthcare providers) certification. Pre-accreditation level certification was granted in April 2016. The key performance indicators to monitor quality of health care also evolved over this period and, currently, reflect more closely patient outcome in the hospital.

5.2 Materials and Method

5.2.1 *ISO Certification*

1. Training: In 2008, once the goal for ISO certification was set, the first step undertaken was creating a pool of internal auditors trained on ISO 9001: 2008 standards who would serve as departmental resource persons for documentation, implementation, and training of the rest of hospital staff. A total of 40 internal auditors drawn from across the hospital (all specialties, administration, and nursing) were trained at Tata Steel SNTI by external faculty, underwent a qualifying test, and were certified as internal auditors.
2. Awareness on ISO standards: A series of awareness classes on ISO standards (Quality Management System ISO 9001: 2008 2009) were conducted by the trained internal auditors to cover all hospital employees. The training program was customized for different employee groups: senior management and departmental heads, medical officers, nursing staff, and ward attendants.

3. Defining responsibility: The General Manager, Medical Services was appointed the Management representative (MR); a Document Control incharge (DCI), an Internal Quality Audit incharge (IQA), and a TQM coordinator were also appointed from amongst the senior hospital doctors.
4. Documentation: The hospital quality manual was written, with defined TMH quality objective. The scope of certification was determined. Procedures were written and were grouped into two categories: common to all and department-specific. The procedures were controlled by the DCI and uploaded on the hospital LAN for easy access, but with defined authority for revision/change of document.
5. Internal audits: A series of internal audits to check implementation and compliance to procedures were carried out by the internal auditors. These were cross-functional audits, with auditors of different specialty auditings for each department.
6. Monitoring of quality systems was through the MR (Management Review) meeting in which the results of internal audits were reviewed.
7. External audits: The external audit for certification was carried out by IRQS in 2009–2010. The stage I audit in March 2009 resulted in a number of nonconformities related to internal audit process and documentation, review mechanism, and infrastructure related. The nonconformities were reviewed in the MR meeting, and specific action plans were drawn with target dates and responsibility (Fig. 5.1, IRQS stage 1 matrix).

The pre-certification audit was conducted in December 2009 and on successful closure of the nonconformities, and the final certification audit was carried out in February 2010. One of the significant nonconformities in the final audit was regarding the hospital statutory and legal requirement TMH was awarded the ISO 9001: 2008 certification in March 2010. However, a review showed NABH

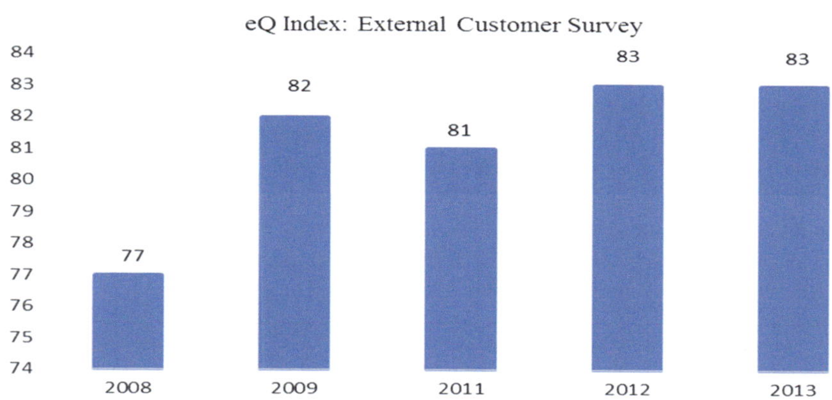

Fig. 5.1 External Customer Satisfaction (eQ) 2008–13

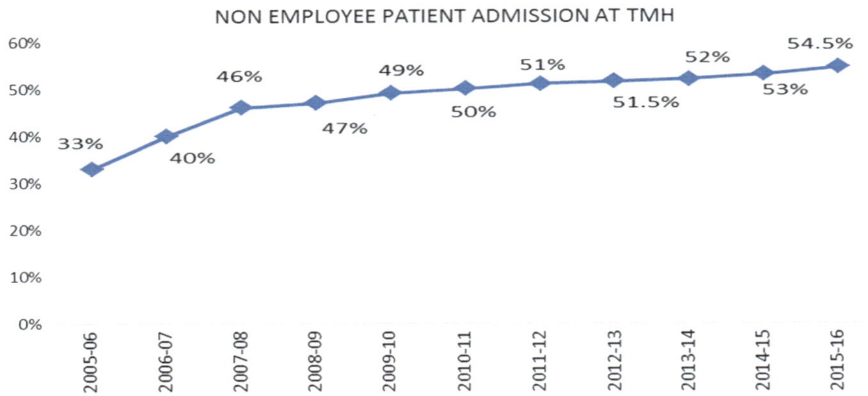

Fig. 5.2 Non-entitled admissions as percentage of total admissions

standards would help the hospital further in its goal to achieve sustained improvement in patient care (Fig. 5.2).

With the background of ISO implementation, adoption of NABH standards was planned in a similar way, but with the idea that there would be a single, integrated quality system followed in the hospital that would incorporate the requirements of both ISO and NABH.

5.2.2 NABH Accreditation

1. Training of core group: In 2010, once again, 42 doctors, nurses, and administration staff underwent the NABH assessors program by NABH faculty, and were examined and issued the internal assessor's certificate. Almost all of these were also ISO internal auditors.
2. Documentation: This was an important area requiring integration since it would be difficult to maintain and control two sets of documents. The ISO quality manual was revised to include NABH standards. New manuals as per NABH standards (Infection Control and Safety) were written and controlled as per ISO document control procedure.

   Forms as per NABH standards were also controlled in document control system. A few examples of noncompliances are given in Table 5.1.

Table 5.1 Representation of noncompliance (as per ISO audit)

Non-compliance	Action plan	Responsibility
In most departments audited, no evidence available to show that corrective actions for identified problems taken after determining root cause	1. Electronic CAPA link to all HODs, internal auditors with lotus notes 2. Training on the module	DCI, TQM coordinator, All HODs
There was no evidence of identification and compliance to statutory regulatory requirements in all areas. Examples: management of biomedical waste, management of solid waste at kitchen, compliance to shops and establishment acts by administration	To list all statutory requirements, control these records through DCS. RMO, All HODs to identify legal requirements in their areas and control it in same manner	RMO, All departments
Criteria for evaluating performance of outsourced processes have not been determined and no evidence that such performance evaluation is carried out	1. Formulation of criteria for evaluation of outsourced agencies 2. Records of performance measurement	Head administration, incharge pathology

3. Process of integration of ISO and NABH quality management system is as follows:

    (i) Top management commitment for NABH accreditation: the Annual Business Plan identified NABH accreditation as one of its objectives.

    (ii) Integration of ISO and NABH hierarchy: The Management Representative was designated NABH counsellor and the TQM coordinator as NABH coordinator. Comparison between ISO and NABH requirements is given in Table 5.2.

    (iii) Creation of NABH committees and core group: The following cross-functional committees were constituted to help in implementation of NABH standards: Apex, CQI (Continuous Quality Improvement), Infection Control, Biomedical waste disposal, Legal, Ethics, Pharmacy, Transfusion, CPR (Cardio-Pulmonary Resuscitation), Internal and Clinical Audit, Medical Records, Disaster, and Safety.

        (a) The CQI committee was headed by the TQM coordinator and included the DCI and IQA incharge. It had also representation from nursing, HR, and customer service.

        (b) Similarly, the internal and clinical audit committees had the IQA as its member.

    (iv) Review mechanisms were integrated by including the review of NABH committee functioning, their performance, and their resource requirements in MR meeting. As the agenda for the review meetings expanded, the MR meeting was split into two parts—the first is to review operational parameters (financial performance, admission, length of stay, etc.) and the second is to focus on internal audits, corrective and preventive

Table 5.2 Comparison between ISO and NABH requirements

Standard/requirement	ISO 9001: 2000	NABH standard	Interpretation
Overall description of processes	Quality manual	Quality, infection, HR, safety manual	Common quality and NABH manual
Leadership and management-related processes	Management responsibility, control of documents responsibility and authority, communication	Responsibilities of management support to quality improvement. Corporate and social responsibility, regulatory requirements	Regulatory and legal requirements MANDATORY for NABH accreditation.
Strategy	Quality management system planning	Covered by responsibilities of management	ABP, KPI formulation, management review
Customer (patient) focus	Customer satisfaction, complaint management	Patient right and education, grievance handling, patient consent, communication with patients	Only consents to be addressed separately
Standard/requirement	ISO 9001: 2008 Standard	NABH standard	Interpretation
Resource management	Employee training, infrastructure, ergonomics	Facility management and safety, HR recruitment, training, Employee safety and health	Training procedure and competency mapping as part of PMS, RECRUITMENT process
Measurement, analysis, and knowledge management	Measurement, analysis, and improvement	Mandatory NABH KPIs	Statistical analysis, audit process, corrective and preventive action, IT process to monitor
Process management	Product and service provision, control of nonconforming services, monitoring and measuring devices	All related to patient care	Admission and discharge process, transfer and referral process, case sheet documentation, lab quality assurance, waste disposal, radiation safety, patient management protocols
Results	Not directly asked-in data analysis and corrective and preventive action	Not directly asked	To be addressed as part of NABH KPI monitoring
Improvement cycle	Continual improvement	Continual improvement	NABH cover ISO and J N Tata requirements barring focus on results

actions, customer complaints, and feedback and review of NABH committees. A total of 24 parameters were reviewed in the first part and 23 in the second part. Parameters suggested by NABH were included as review parameters.

(v) Scope of audit "Curative Health Care" for ISO was enlarged to include specific departments and same was displayed as the scope of services of the hospital.

(vi) Change in document numbering system was done to indicate NABH chapters.

(vii) ISO documents were rearranged with reference to NABH standards.

(viii) Where required, the chairpersons of various NABH committees were given the authority to approve relevant documents.

(ix) ISO clauses were reinterpreted in light of NABH guidelines, e.g., design and development clause for the introduction of new service was interpreted as developing a care plan for each patient.

(x) Clinical audit process, an NABH requirement, was integrated with the self-initiated project (SIP) and corrective and preventive clause of ISO.

4. NABH self-assessment: All NABH requirements were addressed in the ISO internal audits, and thus each internal audit cycle ensured compliance to NABH standards. An NABH and ISO audit checklist was developed and controlled for use during internal audits.
5. Monitoring and review: The procedure on management review was amended to include a review of NABH committee activity, besides the ISO-related review of quality management system.
6. External assessment: An assessment team from another hospital provided the initial, informal feedback on the hospital's preparedness for NABH assessment. The pre-assessment by the NABH assessment team was carried out in December 2013 and the nonconformities closed in March 2014. The final assessment was done in September 2014 and closure was in February 2015. The NABH board went through the assessment report and advised the hospital to improve the nursing strength and address infrastructural issues in the operation theater. In a subsequent verification audit, all remaining nonconformities were closed and pre-accreditation level certification was awarded to the hospital. The infrastructure issues have been addressed and TMH is awaiting another verification audit for full accreditation.

5.2.3 Integration with Tata Steel Daily Management

Tata Steel received the Deming Grand Prize (DGP) in 2012. In line with the Deming philosophy, policy and daily management (DM) was institutionalized right across the organization. TMH integrated the policy and daily management requirements in the existing ISO-NABH quality systems.

Table 5.3 TMH ABP (strategy related to quality)

Strategy	Base FY15	Target FY 16	Responsibility	Means
ISO certification and NABH accreditation	ISO certified	NABH accreditation	GM, medical services, TQM coordinator	Preparation through internal audits

Table 5.4 Evolution of healthcare-specific KPIs

J N Tata KPIs	ISO KPIs	Additional NABH KPIs
Customer satisfaction and complaints	Customer satisfaction and complaints	Out patient and inpatient satisfaction index
OPD and pathology wait time, length of stay, discharge time	OPD and pathology wait time, length of stay, discharge time	Doctor and consultant assessment time, test turnaround time, compliance to case sheet documentation
Income and expenditure	Income and expenditure	Wastage of blood, antibiotic consumption
Bed occupancy	Bed occupancy	CCU and OT utilization
Training man days	Compliance to training plan	Employee engagement score, nurse patient area, adherence to safety precautions
	Errors	Medication errors, adverse anesthesia events, unplanned ventilation, patient falls, proportion of bedsore cases, needle stick injury
		Nosocomial infection

The ABP of the hospital reflected NABH requirements and the Key Performance Indicators (KPI) that cascaded to the various departments therefore ensured that NABH standards were implemented (Table 5.3, TMH ABP).

NABH is required for monitoring 47 performance parameters (related to patient care, safety, cycle times, errors, hospital operational parameters, employee safety and hospital records). These became the DM parameters of TMH monitored at the unit level, through the departmental KPIs and dashboards.

5.3 Results

The KPIs monitored by the hospital are evolved and matured as a result of the observed nonconformity and to address the specific requirements of ISO and NABH (Table 5.4).

(a) **Patient satisfaction results**.
(b) **Customer loyalty results**: The non-entitled patients are a measure of customer loyalty and recall.

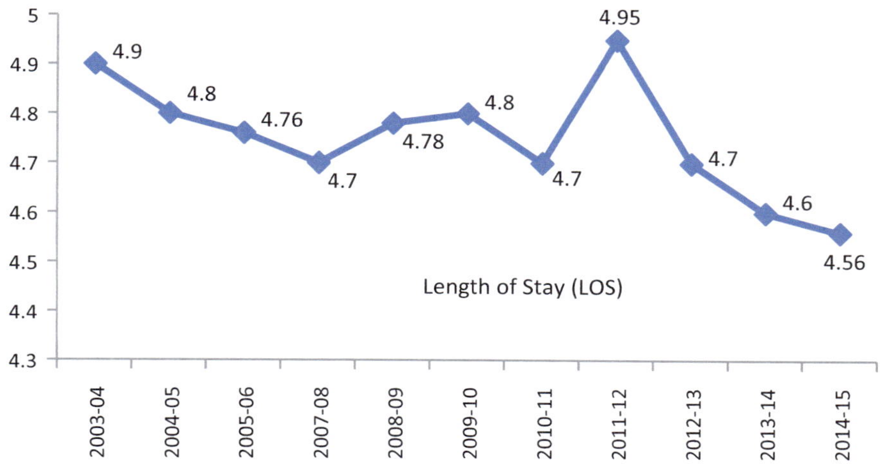

Fig. 5.3 Average Length of Stay (LOS) in days

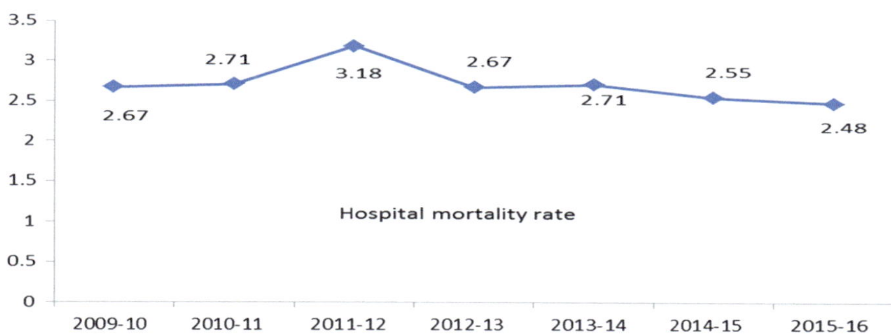

Fig. 5.4 Trend in mortality rate

(c) **Hospital operational results**: The length of stay (LoS) trend is shown in Fig. 5.3.

(d) **Patient care and safety results**: These parameters include response and cycle times, morbidity and mortality figures, hospital infection, etc. Most of these KPIs were put in place after implementation of NABH standards and the results are therefore over 18 months only. The hospital mortality rate is shown in Fig. 5.4. The patient safety status is described in Table 5.5.

(e) **Statutory and legal compliance results**: TMH shows 100% compliance rate on statutory and legal requirements as evidenced in Legatrix, an online monitoring system.

Table 5.5 Patient safety audit results

Critical care areas audited	ICU		CCU		HDU		BCU		PICU	
	Status	Score	Status	Score	Status	Score	Status	Score	Status	Score
Fire safety										
Fire extinguisher present, people know its use, regularly checked	N	0	Y	1	Y	1	Y	1	Y	1
Awareness on patient evacuation drill	N	0	Y	1	Y	1	N	0	N	0
Awareness on fire exit (location and key of exit)	Y	1	Y	1	Y	1	Y	1	N	0
Medication safety										
Awareness about LASA	Y	1	N	0	Y	1	Y	1	Y	1
High risk medication drugs awareness	Y	1	N	0	Y	1	Y	1	N	0
Drug prescription is written in capital letters	N	0	Y	1	N	0	Y	1	Y	1
Errors are recorded	N	0	Y	1	N	0	Y	1	N	0
Surgical safety										
Surgical safety checklist is verbalized	NA	NA	NA	NA	NA	NA	NA	NA	NA	NA
Surgical safety checklist is signed by anaesthesiologist/surgeon/OT nurse	NA	NA	NA	NA	NA	NA	NA	NA	NA	NA
Safety from hospital acquired infection										
Awareness about Handrub and its use	Y	1	Y	1	Y	1	N	0	N	0
Awareness about use of PPE during central line insertion/catheterization	Y	1	Y	1	Y	1	Y	1	Y	1
Safety during transportation of critically ill										
Accompanied by doctor	N	0	Y	1	Y	1	Y	1	Y	1
Availability by oxygen and emergency medication	Y	1	Y	1	Y	1	N	0	N	
Environment safety										
Restraint policy, consent taken	N	0	Y	1	Y	1	N	0	Y	1
Vulnerable tags used	N	0	Y	1	N	0	Y	1	Y	1

(continued)

Table 5.5 (continued)

Critical care areas audited	ICU		CCU		HDU		BCU		PICU	
	Status	Score	Status	Score	Status	Score	Status	Score	Status	Score
Biomedical waste management										
Awareness about waste management policy	N	0	Y	1	Y	1	Y	1	Y	1
Documentation										
Nutritional asessment done and documented	N	0	Y	1	N	0	N	0	Y	1
Prognostication notes signed	Y	1	Y	1	N	0	Y	1	Y	1
Stamp used below signature	N	0	Y	1	N	0	N	0	N	
Date and time is mentioned in doctor's notes	Y	1	Y	1	Y	1	Y	1	Y	1
No abbreviation used for medicine in names	Y	1	Y	1	Y	1			N	
Care plan is documented	N	0	Y	1	N	0	Y	1	Y	1
Regular prognostication and communication is being done	N	0	Y	1	N	0	N	0	N	
Pain assessment id done	Y	1	Y	1	N	0	Y	1	N	
Consents										
Surgical	N	0	Y	1	N	0	Y	1	Y	1
Anesthetic	N	0	Y	1	Y	1	Y	1	Y	1
BT consent	N	0	Y	1	N	0	N	0	N	
Others										
Code blue response	N	0	N		N	0	N	0	Y	1
Critical report register	N	0	Y	1	Y	1	Y	1	Y	1
Patient safety for critical care areas										
Compliance to centre line bundle	N	0	Y	1	N	0	N	0	Y	1
Compliance to VAP bundle	N	0	Y	1	N	0	N	0	Y	1
Compliance to sepsis bundle	N	0	Y	1	N	0	N	0	N	

(continued)

Table 5.5 (continued)

Critical care areas audited	ICU		CCU		HDU		BCU		PICU	
	Status	Score	Status	Score	Status	Score	Status	Score	Status	Score
Managment of patients at risk of aspiration, DVT, stress ulcer	Y	1	Y	1	N	0	N	0	Y	1
Alarms working in area	N	0	Y	1	N	0	N	0	Y	1
Awareness about narcotics/protocol followed	Y	1	Y	1	N	0	N	0	N	0
Score obtained		12		31		16		17		21
% score		38%		97%		50%		53%		66%

5.4 Discussion

The initial approach to improvement in health care through stand-alone quality improvement did not have an impact because of a lack of common goal. The J N Tata model based on Malcolm Baldridge healthcare criteria was an excellence model, with an integrated approach, but implemented prematurely. There was no team approach; protocols and procedures had not been documented; the correct parameters reflecting health care had not been identified; and no measuring system was in place. The J N Tata model therefore could not be sustained and the basics of documentation, measuring, and monitoring and self-assessment had to be first established.

Implementation of ISO 9001: 2008 standard gives a strong documentation base, helped by the online document control system. The strength of ISO was also its internal audit system that ensured regular assessment and review. However, the ISO system lacked implementation of healthcare-related protocol. Patient care-related key performance indicators had not been identified. There was no reference to healthcare-specific infrastructure or human resource requirement of a hospital in the ISO standards.

The process of accreditation to NABH brought in this specific, healthcare-related perspective. The NABH KPI tracker helped to identify, monitor, and improve patient care-related parameters: response time, cycle time, morbidity and mortality, errors and re-do, patient safety, and case sheet documentation. The NABH standards ensured that infrastructures of the hospital, operation theater, CSSD (Central Sterilization Service Department), and critical care units, were built as per standard norms. It ensured that the manpower requirement, in particular, nursing staff, was again as per accepted standard norms.

NABH system does not have an inbuilt periodic and rigorous self-assessment process and review mechanism. Integration with ISO was provided that framework, thus strengthening the review mechanism. An added advantage was the Tata Steel management perspective that brought in the policy and daily management, with the ABP process ensuring goal setting and the daily management process ensuring monitoring of the NABH tracker.

Over two decades, the KPIs were matured from sketchy patient satisfaction survey and few clinical parameters to the present NABH tracker that covers the entire gamut of patient care and safety in a hospital.

The results reflect this maturity. The length of stay, an overall measurement of the efficiency of the hospital processes (diagnosis and treatment time), has shown a significant fall. There is fall in the hospital mortality rate. The number of non-entitled patients, reflecting the non-captive group, has steadily increased. The integration of ISO and NABH requirements brought together the best of both systems. Some of the unique practices put in place as a result were the patient safety audits, combined audit checklists and an integrated review mechanism. The other unique approach was to involve hospital staff in the journey. It ensured ownership and better understanding of processes as well as provide empowerment.

The way forward is to further refine morbidity parameters and adopt an overall hospital index reflecting patient outcome like the hospital standardized mortality rate.

5.5 Conclusion

By adopting an integrated approach to quality improvement, Tata Main hospital ensured a greater impact on patient care. The best practices of ISO system—documentation, internal audits, and review—were combined with the patient care centric standards of NABH. The approach also integrated Tata Steel's policy and daily management. The involvement of hospital staff helped to ensure sustainability.

Acknowledgements We wish to thank the General Manager, Medical Services, Tata Steel for permission to publish our study.

References

Health Care Criteria for Performance Excellence, Baldridge National Quality Program (2001).

Mitra, S. (2001a). Tools of total quality management, Health Administrator, Vols. xi and xii.

Mitra, S. (2001b). An introduction to TATA business excellence model, Health Administrator, Vols. xi and xii.

National Accreditation Board for Hospital and Healthcare Providers (NABH). (2011). *Accreditation standards for hospitals* (3rd ed.).

Quality Management System ISO 9001: 2008. (2009). *Total quality management Tata steel* (4th ed.).

Chapter 6
A Study on Redesigning Modern Healthcare Using Internet of Things

K. Rajeswari, N. Vivekanandan, P. Amitaraj and Ajay Fulambarkar

Abstract In today's fast world owing to advancement in medical technology, health care has become one of the most striking application areas for the Internet of Things (IoT). There is a huge competition in building up high-speed healthcare services. The IoT has the perspective to offer many medical applications such as remote health monitoring, elder care, and chronic diseases especially heart disease monitoring and emergency support for the needy people. The study suggests a system that will improve the performance of health care even in the rural areas. Tracking patient's location, sensing parameters like blood pressure, glucose, breathing rate and automatic data collection, and analysis of the data will take the IoT to the next level of healthcare applications. State-of-the-art IoT healthcare system built with Decision Support System (DSS) will definitely help the patients and doctors in critical conditions. Proposed work targets Ischemic Heart Disease (IHD) with IoT application.

Keywords Health care · Internet of things (IoT) · Decision support system (DSS) · Ischemic heart disease (IHD)

K. Rajeswari (✉)
Department of Computer Engineering, Pimpri Chinchwad College of Engineering, Pune, India
e-mail: kannan.rajeswari@pccoepune.org; raji.pccoe@gmail.com

N. Vivekanandan
Department of Mechanical Engineering, Pimpri Chinchwad College of Engineering, Pune, India

P. Amitaraj
Cardio Thoracic Department, Madras Medical College, Chennai, Tamilnadu, India

A. Fulambarkar
Pimpri Chinchwad College of Engineering, Pune, India

P.K. Ray and J. Maiti (eds.), *Healthcare Systems Management: Methodologies and Applications*, Managing the Asian Century,
DOI 10.1007/978-981-10-5631-4_6

6.1 Introduction

The Internet of Things (IoT) is a term which means connect everyone, everything, every service, and every network anytime and any place. Modern health care is one of the most important applications of IoT (Pang 2013). The IoT has the perspective to offer many medical applications such as remote health monitoring, elder care, and chronic diseases especially heart disease monitoring and emergency support for the needy people.

Personalization of health care and connectivity with doctors and hospitals is the latest trend in health care. IoT supports this trend by connecting everything all time and in all places including remote areas. Medical devices like personal home-use diagnostic devices and imaging devices that are used by mobile health workers are one of the key technology components (Khanna and Misra 2016).

Connected healthcare technology will help in reducing the occurrence of chronic diseases like heart disease and diabetes by continuous monitoring of patients by doctors, with data analytics using decision support system. IoT-based connected healthcare system sets up an environment where vital parameters are sensed by devices like sensors, transmitted through a gateway, and stored in a cloud where aggregation and analysis of data happen with the appropriate decision support system. Figure 6.1 gives an overview of healthcare trends with IoT.

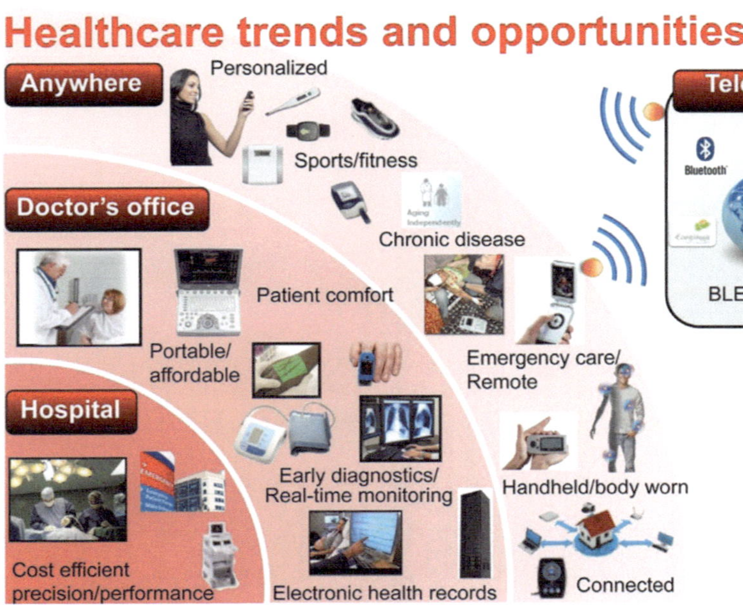

Fig. 6.1 Healthcare trends with IoT (Vasanth and Sbert 2016)

Further, in this paper, Sect. 6.2 provides literature available in health care and IoT, Sect. 6.3 discusses example use cases, Sect. 6.4 provides details about data analytic techniques, Sect. 6.5 discusses proposed work, and Sect. 6.6 concludes the paper.

6.2 Literature on Health Care and IoT

Begum and Venugopal (2016) have discussed the importance of monitoring the health of patients on daily basis. An effective modernized healthcare system is required to keep every individual healthy (Abdullah et al. 2015). In their paper, they have discussed the implementation of wireless health monitoring system. The components used were ECG electrodes, LM35 temperature sensor, blood pressure sensor, Microsoft pro tablet, and blood glucose sensor. IoT helps in tracking the patient health parameters, connects with doctor, and keeps track of patient records in detail through the use of sensors, detectors, actuators, etc. (Yehia et al. 2015). Yvette et al. have discussed Ubiquitous healthcare system where people need not visit hospital to monitor their health. It promises accuracy and availability of medical treatment online (Gelogo et al. 2015). The main parts of U-Healthcare system are as follows:

(a) Body area network which has sensors attached to the body to capture body bio signals, body temperature, pulse, etc.
(b) Intelligent medical server which has analytics module to determine if the patient is in critical condition or not.
(c) Hospital system where nurses/doctors will take corrective actions based on patient report.

Such systems not only help patients, but also healthcare professionals from moving from one place to another. When a patient is in unstable state, the sensors will warn practitioners/nurse remotely in order to help them (Konstantinidis et al. 2015).

Gupta et al. (2016) have suggested Internet of Things Analytics (IoTA) to handle a large collection of data generated and analyze them effectively. They have proposed an intelligent, robust healthcare management system to monitor the patient effectively and automatically. The status information is collected through systems automatically. Blood pressure, heart rate, and ECG are the parameters collected and sent as an emergency alert to medical practitioner with revised status and complete patient information. It uses smart sensors generating raw data collected from each sensor and sends it to a database server where the data is analyzed statistically and maintained to be used by the medical team. Maintenance of a database server is necessary to keep an eye of previous record of the patient for a better and improved examination.

Cooey (2016) uses Bluetooth to log in medical data of patients. The system gives alerts on health risks to patients. It connects with pharma, labs, doctors, and tele-consulting. It has Smart Blood Pressure Monitor, Glucometer, and Body Analyzer.

It has a personalized healthcare monitoring system. Cooey smart services help chronic patients to survive. Microsoft Health Vault (2016) assists the patient to collect, store, utilize, and share health information. All health records can be maintained at one place and are available online. Especially during medical emergencies it helps to keep track of all the details. Data is recorded once, and used with new data to get frequent updates about health. It has multiple application connectivities to share the information with everyone.

Key Characteristics:

- Updated medication;
- Updated readings of blood pressure, glucose level, and weight from home;
- History of health details; and
- HealthVault to store, organize, and share the data with doctor.

This provides easy information to healthcare consultants for advising the user on proper health management. Dashboard of weight management guides the user to have fitness watching the weight, daily diet, physical activity, and tracking the progress always.

6.3 Use Cases on Health Care and IoT

The IoT is a boon to the society in terms of 3D's namely Disease, Data, Devices[1] (Krawiec et al. 2015). Here, the authors have mentioned that most IoT-enabled devices are wearables like activity monitors and devices like digital scales and thermometers and an application to track results. IoT applications promise to improve and personalize patient healthcare by making everything automatic. The interactions with patients are periodic. In the United States, everyday behaviors cause conditions causing about 40% of premature deaths.[2] If the digitally collected patient data is reliable, then IoT applications can critically improve personalized health care (Dale and Hagen 2007). Remote patient monitoring will save up to $36 billion globally in the next 5 years (Deering 2013). Specifically, home monitoring has the possibility to decrease the incidence of death and hospitalization occurred by falls (Beltrone 2014; Shany et al. 2012). IoT-based home monitoring devices can reduce costs, improving outcomes by preventing falls. This is by predicting the likelihood of a fall with data acquisition and decision support system by observing movements and pressure distribution (Igual et al. 2013).

---

[1]Mathias Cousin, Tadashi Castillo—Hi, Glenn H. Synder, Devices and diseases: How the IoT is transforming medtech. http://dupress.deloitte.com/dup-us-en/focus/internet-of-things/iot-in-medical-devices-industry.html#endnote-sup-5.

[2]http://allthingsd.com/20130529/mary-meekers-internet-trends-report-is-back-at-d11-slides/ (accessed 1 October, 2016).

Use case: Care at Home

Current status and

Elderly individuals who are at risk of health are placed in the full-time care of relatives, nurses, or old age homes.

Use of IoT:

- Detecting slips (Patel et al. 2012), and
- Checking if an individual took his/her medicine (West 2012)

Other use cases of IoT include

- Care for the kids,
- Chronic disease management,
- Personal health and fitness management, and
- Short-term care planning to give medicines by keeping reminders.

6.4 Data Analytic Techniques

Wu et al. (2002) have proposed a combination of decision support system with computer-based data mining techniques to reduce the medical errors, improve patient's safety, reduce the unwanted practices, and increase patients' true positive and true negative outcome. Ouardighi et al. (2007) proposed a feature selection method based on Wilk's Lambda criterion. It is a statistical method used in discriminant analysis. Correlation-based feature selection is used by Umut and Fikret (Arıkan and Gürgen 2012) for Arrhythmia classification. Twenty-two attributes were selected giving good accuracy with different classifiers like Bayes classifier, support vector machines, neural networks (MLP), and C4.5 Decision tree classifiers. Agarwal and Srikant (1994) have dealt with this issue in depth and proposed a new approach that adopts subset lattice search space, using structural properties of frequent item sets to assist fast detection. Association algorithms find interrelationships between data and reveal this relationship in the form of rules. The efficiency of them is one of the key distinguishers in the midst of different algorithms. Several algorithms build a database of rules, confidence factors, and support to facilitate querying (For example, "illustrate all associations where computer is the consequent, with a confidence factor of over 90% with a support of 80% or more"). According to Borgelt and Kruse (2002), association analysis is a powerful method to generate association rules for market basket analysis to understand the customer's behavior while shopping. In data mining, classification is one of the important problems. As stated by Xu-min liu et al. (2006), in a given database, each record with a class label, a classifier produces a concise and meaningful description of each class that can be used to classify subsequent records. Han and Kamber

(2001) explain the rule-based classification approach as follows. A better way to represent information is by using Rules. Rule induction is a process for obtaining a set of rules to classify cases. If-Then rules are used in rule-based classifier system. The rules can be generated either from decision or from training data using sequential covering algorithm. Though decision trees produce a set of rules, rule induction methods produce a set of independent rules that do not essentially from a tree. Parthiban and Subramanian (2008) have proposed an innovative approach based on Coactive Neuro-Fuzzy Inference System (CANFIS) to predict heart disease. The presence of the disease is diagnosed by the CANFIS model. Ganji and Abadeh (2010) have used Ant Colony Optimization (ACO) to extract a set of rules for diagnosis of diabetes. It extracts fuzzy If-Then rules for diagnosis. Innocent et al. (1997) have experimented with fuzzy neural networks. Experience acquired using fuzzy neural networks is modeled and used in the improvement of classification accuracy.

Many hybrid techniques with data analytics were proposed and implemented. Ahmad et al. (2013) have implemented a hybrid combination of Artificial Neural Networks (ANN) and genetic algorithm. Pandey and Mishra (2009) have made a literature survey of all hybrid methods available for intelligent computing in medical planning, diagnosis, and treatment. Li (2006) confirmed that Intelligent Information Processing is a field of research for the past 10–15 years. To address the problems and to focus on this research area, an International Conference on Intelligent Information Processing was held at Beijing in 2006. Many research works presented in the conference dealt with genetic algorithm, fuzzy logic, and case-based reasoning. Companies are investing more money for retrieving intelligent information from a large collection of data. Tang et al. (1999) have discussed the intelligent processing of medical images by having a prior knowledge about the medical domain for analysis. According to their papers, Knowledge-Based Systems (KBS) consist of Rule-Based Reasoning (RBR), Case-Based Reasoning (CBR), Model-Based Reasoning (MBR), Intelligent Computing Method (ICM) encompasses Genetic Algorithm (GA), Artificial Neural Networks (ANN), Fuzzy Logic (FL), and others. The hybrid methods such as CBR-RBR, CBR-MBR and RBR-CBR-MBR, ANN-GA, Fuzzy-ANN, Fuzzy-GA and Fuzzy-ANN-GA, RBR-ANN, CBR-ANN, RBR-CBR-ANN, Fuzzy-RBR, Fuzzy-CBR, and Fuzzy-CBR-ANN are very useful.

Neural networks are nonparametric, robust, and exhibit good learning and generalization abilities in data-rich environments. Genetic algorithms present competent search algorithms to choose a model, from mixed media data, based on several preference criteria/objective functions. Rough sets are rightly used for handling various types of uncertainty in data. Sivagaminathan and Ramakrishnan (2007) have described a hybrid method to select a subset of features. Variables contributing for noise and strongly correlated with a selected variable are removed. Combination of ant colony optimization and neural networks is used as a hybrid technique.

6.5 Proposed Work

Ischemic Heart Disease (IHD) is a chronic disease which is topping the death reason in countries like India (Rajeswari and Vaithiyanathan 2011). Sudden death occurs when some of the health parameters are not regularly monitored. This work focuses on regular monitoring of parameters of individuals especially in rural areas where there is acute shortage of doctors especially cardiologists. Figure 6.2 shows the framework of the system (Vuorinen et al. 2014).

The attributes to be collected from patients in three stages are listed in Tables 6.1, 6.2, and 6.3. These attributes are finalized in discussion with Madras Medical College. A mobile application is used to upload all the measurements. The risk for IHD are classified as no risk, low risk , medium risk and high risk as shown in Table 6.4.

A software mobile application is proposed to get the parameters listed in Stage 1, 2, and 3. In rural areas, Primary Health Care (PHC) centers generally help people

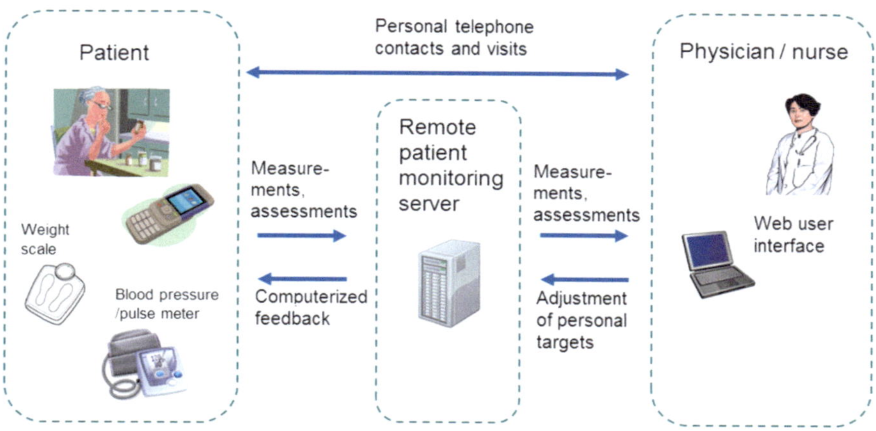

Fig. 6.2 Continuous monitoring of patients with chronic disease

Table 6.1 Stage 1 of data for IHD

Stage 1						
1. Age	2. Sex	3. Menopause	4. Height	5. Weight	6. Body Mass Index	7. Waist Measure

Table 6.2 Stage 2—Comorbid factors of IHD

Stage 2				
Comorbid factors				
8. SBP	9. DBP	10. Diabetes	11. Cholesterol	12. Thyroid

Table 6.3 Stage 3 of data for IHD

Stage 3				
12. Personal habits Y (Pang 2013)/ N[0]	13. Family history Y[1]/ N[0]	14. Genetic factors Y[1]/ N[0]	15. TypeA personality Y[1]/N[0]	16. Sleeping disturbance Y[1]/N[0]

Table 6.4 Risk for IHD

Absolute Risk for IHD			
No risk	Low risk	Medium risk	High risk

for basic medical issues. In this work we propose to take the measurements with the help of supporting staff present there. The patients will be advised to report the measurements once a week. Parameters like age need to be orally asked to patients parameters like Systolic blood pressure (SBP) can be measured with Pressure measuring machine. Initially, based on the parameters collected risk of the patient is classified by experts, based on their experience. To make the system critical, it is suggested to have minimum three expert opinions. In case of contradiction, the class label value is the maximum. This data collected along with the class label will be analyzed by decision support system and in case of critical cases (High risk), doctors and ambulance services will be informed to support the patient immediately. Patients with low risk and medium risk will be advised to visit doctors and take medications with diet recommendations. If recommendations are not followed reminder/warning messages will be given to the patient and the relative(s). Based on the recommendation, few of the Stage 1, 2, and 3 parameters need to be collected on every visit (weekly/monthly). Few parameters may be static and automatically updated (like age). The proposed system will reduce the number of sudden death of patients due to IHD especially in rural areas as continuously health parameters are monitored.

6.6 Challenges

This work to implement in rural India is a big challenge mainly due to the following reasons:

1. People have to report to PHC weekly (or at least monthly;
2. Cost of Equipment. Approximately 23,236 healthcare centers are there in India (2016). Costs of different equipments are given in Table 6.5.

In a single PHC, at least two sets of equipment are to be kept (one for male and other for female);

Table 6.5 Unit cost to select medical equipment (in Rupees)

Sr no	Type of Equipment	Cost per unit
1	Weighing machine	Rs 3000
2	Height measuring machine	Rs 3000
3	Pressure machine	Rs 1500
4	Diabetes measuring machine	Rs 1000
5	Cholesterol measuring machine	Rs 3000
6	Thyroid checking machine	Rs 5000
7	Total approximate cost (Minimum)	Rs 16,500

3. Ability to operate and maintain medical devices;
4. Creating relevant databases and use of analytical tools and techniques supporting the requirements of physicians as well as the patients; and
5. Security of data to be used for cloud computing.

6.7 Conclusion

The paper has presented the details of the state-of-the-art tools and techniques required to be used for designing and operating a healthcare system using IoT platform. Further, the paper proposes a system for reducing the death ratio due to IHD especially in rural areas. In noncritical cases, medicines can also be delivered to the rural addresses if pharmaceutical companies are connected with IoT with the prescription of medical practitioners. As a result, a set of recommendations to maintain the health of an individual in terms of the followingadvices on physical exercises, task scheduling, use of relaxation methods like hearing music, laughing loud, viewing comedy shows, watching movies, etc., as a part of healthcare system may bring a positive attitudinal change and transformation in health status among individuals in healthcare domain. Redesigning the healthcare systems with IoT, especially in rural areas of India, would help overcome many challenges to build and sustain an effective healthcare system in India.

References

Abdullah, A., Ismael, A., Rashid, A., Abou-ElNour, A, & Tarique, M. (2015), Real time health monitoring application using mobile devices. *IJCNC, 7*(3).

Agrawal, R., & Srikanth, R. (1994). Fast algorithms for mining association rules. In *Proceedings of 20th International Conference on Very Large Data Bases*.

Ahmad, F., Mat Isa, N. A., Hussain, Z., & Osman, M. K. (2013). Intelligent medical disease diagnosis using improved genetic algorithm—multilayer perceptron network. *Journal of Medical Systems, 37*(2), 9934.

Arıkan, U., & Gürgen, F. (2012). Discrimination ability of time-domain features and rules for arrhythmia classification. *Mathematical and Computational Applications, 17*(2), 111–120.

Begum, S., & Venugopal. (2016). Comparison of various techniques in IoT for health care system. *International Journal of Computer Science and Mobile Computing, 5*(3), 59–66.

Beltrone, G. (2014). Life alert's new ad is terrifying, and people are not happy about it, AdWeek. www.adweek.com/adfreak/life-alerts-new-ad-terrifying-and-viewers-are-not-happy-about-it-159750. Accessed October 1, 2016.

Borgelt, C., & Kruse, R. (2002). *Induction of association rules: Apriori implementation* (pp. 395–400). Compstst: Physica-Verlag.

Dale, O., & Hagen, K. B. (2007). Despite technical problems personal digital assistants outperform pen and paper when collecting patient diary data. *Journal of Clinical Epidemiology, 60*(1), 8–17.

Deering, M. J. (2013). Patient-generated health data and health IT, Office of the National Coordinator for Health IT. www.healthit.gov/sites/default/files/pghd_brief_final122013.pdf. Accessed October 1, 2016.

Ganji, M. F., & Abadeh, M. S. (2010). Using fuzzy ant colony optimization for diagnosis of diabetes disease. In *18th Iranian Conference on Electrical Engineering* (*ICEE*) (pp. 501–505). IEEE.

Gelogo, Y. E., Hwang, H. J., & Kim, H.-K. (2015). Internet of Things (IoT) Framework for u-healthcare System. *International Journal of Smart Home, 9*(11).

Gupta, P., Agrawal, D., Chhabra, J., & Dhir, P. K. (2016). IoT based Smart healthcare kit. In *IEEE International Conference on Computational Techniques in Information and Communication Technologies*.

Han, J., & Kamber, M. (2001). *Datamining: Concepts and techniques*. San Francisco, CA: Morgan Kaufmann Publishers.

https://cooey.co.in/. Accessed October 1, 2016.

https://www.healthvault.com/in/en/overview. Accessed October 1, 2016.

https://www.ncbi.nlm.nih.gov/pmc/articles/PMC4014652/. Accessed November 1, 2016.

Igual, R., Medrano, C., Plaza, I. (2013). Challenges, issues and trends in fall detection systems . *Biomedical Engineering, 12*.

Innocent, P. R., Barnes, M. R., & John, R. I. (1997). Application of the fuzzy ART/MAP and MinMax/MAP neural network models to radiographic image classificatio. *Artificial Intelligence in Medicine, 11*(3), 241–263.

Khanna, A., & Misra, P. (2016). The Internet of Things for medical devices prospects, challenges and the way forward. `Online]. Available at: http://www.tcs.com/SiteCollectionDocuments/White%20Papers/Internet-of-Things-Medical-Devices_0714-2.pdf. Accessed October 1, 2016.

Konstantinidis, E. I., Bamparopoulos, G., Billis, A., & Bamidis, P. D. (2015). Internet of Things for an age-friendly healthcare.

Krawiec, R. J., Nadler, J., Tye, E., & Jarboe, J. (2015). No appointment necessary: How the IoT and patient generated data can unlock health care value. http://dupress.deloitte.com/dup-us-en/focus/internet-of-things/iot-in-health-care-industry.html#endnote-sup-52. Accessed October 1, 2016.

http://allthingsd.com/20130529/mary-meekers-internet-trends-report-is-back-at-d11-slides/. Accessed October 1, 2016.

Li, Xu. (2006a). Advances in intelligent information processing. *Expert Systems, 23*(5), 249–250.

Li, Xu. (2006b). Advances in intelligent information processing. *Expert Systems, 23*(5), 249–250.

Yehia, L., Khedr, A., & Darwish, A. (2015). Hybrid security techniques for internet of things healthcare applications. *Advances in Internet of Things, 5*, 21–25.

Ouardighi, E. I., Akadi, E. I., & Aboutajdine, D (2007). Feature selection on supervised classification using Wilk's lambda statistic. In *3rd International Symposium on Computational Intelligence and Intelligent Informatics—ISCIII* (pp. 51–55). IEEE.

Pandey, B., & Mishra, R. B. (2009). Knowledge and intelligent computing system in medicine. *Computers in Biology and Medicine, 39*(3), 215–230.

Pang, Z (2013, January), *Technologies and architectures of the Internet-of-Things* (*IoT*) *for health and well-being* (M.S. thesis). Department of Electronic and Computer System, KTH-Roy. Institute of Technology, Stockholm, Sweden.

Parthiban, L., & Subramanian, R. (2008). Intelligent heart disease prediction system using CANFIS and genetic algorithm. *International Journal of Biological, Biomedical and Medical Sciences, 3*(3), 157–160.

Patel, S., Park, H., Bonato, P., Chan, L., & Rodgers, M. (2012). A review of wearable sensors and systems with application in rehabilitation. *Journal of neuroengineering and rehabilitation, 9*(1), 1.

Rajeswari, K., & Vaithiyanathan, V. (2011). Heart disease diagnosis: An efficient decision support system based on fuzzy logic and genetic algorithm. *International Journal of Decision Sciences, Risk and Management, 3*, 81–97.

Shany, T., Redmond, S. J., Narayanan, M. R., & Lovell, N. H. (2012). Sensors-based wearable systems for monitoring of human movement and falls. *IEEE Sensors Journal, 12*(3), 658–670.

Sivagaminathan, R. K., & Ramakrishnan, S. (2007). A hybrid approach for feature subset selection using neural networks and ant colony optimization. *Expert Systems with Applications, 33*(1), 49–60.

Tang, L. H. Y., Hanka, R., & Horace, H. S. (1999). A review of intelligent content-based indexing and browsing of medical images. *Health Informatics Journal., 5*(1), 40–49.

Vasanth, K, & Sbert, J. (2016). Creating solutions for health through technology innovation. Texas Instruments. [Online] available at: http://www.ti.com/lit/wp/sszy006/sszy006.pdf. Accessed October 1, 2016.

Vuorinen, A.-L., Leppänen, J., Kaijanranta, H., Kulju, M., Heliö, T., van Gils, M., et al. (2014). Use of home telemonitoring to support multidisciplinary care of heart failure patients in finland: randomized controlled trial. *Journal of Medical Internet Research.*

West, D. (2012). How mobile devices are transforming healthcare. *Issues in Technology Innovation, 18*(1), 1–11.

Wu, R., Peters, W., & Morgan, M. W. (2002). The next generation clinical decision support: Linking evidence to best practice. *Journal Health care Information Management, 16*(4), 50–55.

Chapter 7
Inventory Management and Analysis of Pharmaceuticals in a Healthcare System

Esha Saha and Pradip Kumar Ray

Abstract In a healthcare system, predominantly in hospital systems, varieties of patient with distinct medical condition visit in search of care and treatment. A typical multispecialty hospital system consists of various departments like cardiology, neurology, gynecology, ophthalmology, etc., for the treatment of various patients with various medical conditions ranging from less critical conditions like fever, infections, fracture, etc., to extremely critical conditions like ischemic heart diseases, chronic obstructive pulmonary disease, urinary tract infection, etc. Thus, a hospital system with various departments/specialties appoints various specialized physicians in each domain, and maintains large quantity and variety of physician preference pharmaceutical products in the hospital inpatient pharmacy unit for both scheduled and emergency patients. Depending on the medical condition of patients and specialty, inpatient pharmacy maintains inventory of set of medicines, such as medicines acting on the respiratory tract, cardiovascular medicines, medicines affecting blood, anesthetics, analgesics/antipyretics, anti-allergics and medicines used in anaphylaxis, antidotes, anti-infective items, plasma substitutes, dermatological medicines, diuretics, gastrointestinal medicines, vitamins and minerals, medicines acting on ear, nose and oropharynx which are dispensed to wards, operating theaters, critical care units, and other department within the hospitals. Based on the timeliness of administering the medicines, the set of medicines are classified with the characteristics that the patients requiring medicines without any delay are the most critical patient and so on. Therefore, depending on the criticality of patient condition and specialty/department, set of medicines are classified. The number of patients in a hospital unit at a particular time and their medical condition and reaction to treatment during their length-of-stay is random and changes with time, so the demand of required medicines is stochastic and highly uncertain. Thus, the classification of medicines helps in determining the demand pattern and distribution of each classes and the corresponding inventory strategy for them in order to optimize the hospital inpatient pharmacy inventory so that right quantity of

E. Saha (✉) · P.K. Ray
Department of Industrial and Systems Engineering, Indian Institute of Technology, Kharagpur 721302, India
e-mail: eshasaha83@gmail.com

P.K. Ray and J. Maiti (eds.), *Healthcare Systems Management: Methodologies and Applications*, Managing the Asian Century,
DOI 10.1007/978-981-10-5631-4_7

medicines are available at right time considering the constraints and conditions of a typical hospital system. Thus, the characteristics, such as arrival rate, transferal and discharge rates, demand distribution, list of medicines, their administration time, etc., need to be analyzed for which relevant data are collected through observations, hospital information system records and discussion with expert medical personnel and hospital administration of a multispecialty hospital in India. The purpose of the paper is to introduce the applicability of classification of pharmaceuticals based on the patient medical condition within the environment of a hospital inpatient pharmacy for improving the performance of inventory management system in hospitals.

Keywords Inventory management · Patient medical condition · Medicines · Multispecialty hospitals

7.1 Introduction

A hospital inventory comprises of large number and great variety of items for the proper treatment and care of patients, such as pharmaceuticals, medical equipments, surgical items, etc. A study on health care is encouraged with the prime motive of enhancing the service level of patient. To meet the regular demand of the patient, the healthcare units need to be always prepared with the required resources so that no delay hinders the treatment of the patients who may arrive in any extreme health condition. Along with meeting regular demand, resources for handling emergency situations must be efficient in the healthcare units to provide maximum service to the patients arriving unscheduled in highly critical condition. To maintain all the necessary resources to fulfill the regular and emergency demand of patients, inventory of items required for patient treatment needs to be available at the right place and at the right time (Saha and Ray 2016).

With the dynamic patient condition, distinctive procedures are required to treat the patients, consequently, huge amount of and great varieties of items are needed for treating them, but traditionally less attention was given in managing the inventories in healthcare setting (Nicholson et al. 2004). But, with the continual tight budget allocation for healthcare and constant pressure from stakeholders for cost minimization, a tradeoff between inventory-related cost and service level is needed and unnecessary investment in inventory need to be controlled (de Vries 2011). Mainly, healthcare units experience inventory-related problems when lot of money is tied in the overstocked inventory along with the workforce and space for maintaining that stock (Little and Coughlan 2008; Kelle et al. 2012). As a result, efficient inventory management system is encouraged for managing and controlling various healthcare resource inventories for the smooth running of the healthcare units. The demand in a hospital setting is mostly considered to be independent demand as it is mainly concerned with finished goods. But, certain items need to be produced from the raw materials in the hospital having compounding facilities where the demand of raw material depends on the demand of finished goods, i.e., dependent demand (Vila-Parrish et al. 2012). Generally, the authors assume stationary demand but it is observed that the demand of hospital inventory items is non-stationary, i.e., the demand distribution changes with the change in the number of patients in a unit with time (Vila-Parrish et al. 2012). The demand in hospital depends on the patients' characteristics which changes stochastically.

Stochastic demand with fixed lead time is assumed while modelling by Guerrero et al. (2013). Consideration of stochastic demand and variable lead time while modelling inventory problem is more close to real situation in a healthcare facility (Attanayake et al. 2014; Uthayakumar and Priyan 2013). Continuous Review with control parameters order quantity and reorder point (Roni et al. 2015), and Periodic Review with control parameters review period and maximum inventory level (Gebicki et al. 2014; Satir and Cengiz 1987) are the common replenishment policies considered in an inventory problem. Various combinations of control parameters are also being applied (Guerrero et al. 2013). The objective of this paper is to study the various ways the pharmaceutical items may be classified in a hospital to make inventory-related decisions. This paper discusses in the following subsections the various complexities and unique characteristics of pharmaceutical inventory management.

7.1.1 Complexities in Pharmaceutical Inventory Management

The various complexities in pharmaceutical inventory management are the stochastic nature of the problem, heterogeneity of patient, patient and item criticality, demand variability and uncertainty, price variability, return of item after issuance due to change in the patient condition, perishability of the pharmaceutical items, physician preference items, substitutable items, personal hiding places, inaccuracy in recording data, tending to order more in the fear of shortages, uniqueness and peculiarity of individual hospitals, etc. According to Joint Commission on Accreditation of Healthcare Organizations (JCAHO), the primary objective of healthcare inventory management is to ensure delivering right dose of right medication to right patient at right time through right route. Each medication has a required service level that is dependent on its criticality, a measure of consequences of a stockout, possibly death of a patient.

7.1.2 Characteristics of Pharmaceutical Inventory Management

The unique characteristics of pharmaceutical inventory management include low and uncertain demand with high price items that are maintained in stock to avoid costly consequences of not having those in stock during patient treatment and care.

Thus, managing pharmaceutical inventories in hospitals is challenging because ensuring 100% service level is the primary objective with cost minimization as secondary objective. The pharmaceutical inventory management in hospitals is unique since it considers the interrelationship between the patient's condition and item utilization. Each pharmaceutical item has a required service level that is dependent on patient condition criticality. The measure of the consequences of a stockout in case of pharmaceuticals may be even death of a patient. Additional constraints of pharmaceuticals include their perishable nature which is high for intravenous liquids and limited availability in cases when the lead times for items vary. Consequently, pharmaceutical item availability may affect the patient condition leading to longer hospital stay which may have an impact in its demand.

7.2 Review of Literature

In healthcare systems, predominantly in hospitals, pharmaceutical distribution is designed as multi-echelon inventory system. A central store receives the items from the external suppliers. The central store is closely connected to the central pharmacy being in charge of procurement and inventory management of the pharmaceuticals. The central pharmacy regularly delivers to the point-of-use inventories that are located close to the patient care locations, such as emergency rooms, wards, intensive care units, high dependency units, diagnostic units, laboratory units, and operating theaters. The relevant literature as described in the following subsections includes the literature on inventory models and control policies and classification of pharmaceutical items.

7.2.1 Inventory Models and Control Policies

This section presents the literature regarding types of inventory models (static and dynamic) and control policies (continuous and periodic). In case of static inventory models, only one order is possible, whereas in dynamic inventory models, more than one order is possible. These models can further be classified into static and dynamic models under certainty, risk and uncertainty based on the characteristics of demand. The main concern is to select suitable inventory policy, which comprises of inventory review cycle (continuous/periodic), and their corresponding inventory parameter settings (reorder level and order quantity in case of continuous review policy and review period and maximum inventory level in case of periodic review period, and at times combinations). Most publications apply a periodic inventory review policy and such policy is generally practiced in hospitals. But in healthcare settings, due to uncertainty of patient arrivals and resulting demand, continuous review policy is more applicable. The maintained inventory levels in the hospital depend on the physicians' and nurses' desire rather than computed parameters.

7.2.1.1 Aspects of Inventory Problem

The two main aspects of the inventory problem are the future demand and the lead time. The knowledge of future demand and lead time may be categorized into the following three categories of inventory problems:

(a) Inventory Problems under Certainty

In case of scheduled patents and treatment and/or tests procedures, the future demand may be known with certainty; however, due to the change in the patient condition due to the treatment, the demand for medication and/or medical supplies may vary.

(b) Inventory Problems under Risk

In case of inventory problems under risk, the probability distribution of demand is likely to be available, i.e., the records of past demand of the pharmaceutical items are available.

(c) Inventory Problems under Uncertainty

In the case of inventory problem under uncertainty, the probability distribution of demand of pharmaceutical items is unknown or uncertain, i.e., entirely unaware of the likelihood of various levels of future demand.

In case of dynamic inventory problems, the demand may be stationary, i.e., constant probability distribution of demand and may be non-stationary, i.e., probability distribution of demand varies over time.

The lead time is the time lag between the time when an order is placed and the time when the order is received. For certain kinds of inventory problems, this time lag is essentially constant whereas, for other kinds of inventory problems there is a probability distribution of possible time lags.

7.2.1.2 Inventory Control Systems

Inventory may be managed by periodic (P-system), continuous (Q-system) review processes and combination review processes. In a continuous review system, a decision is made to order or not to order a replenishment quantity whenever the value of inventory position changes. An order is placed whenever the inventory position reaches a reorder point. In a periodic review system, the inventory position or the inventory level is checked at regularly scheduled times. The review period is the time interval between reviews. Periodic review generally is used with slow-moving items whereas continuous review is for fast moving items or whenever inexpensive processes exist for checking the state of the inventory.

Continuous Review Systems

The continuous review systems (Q-system) have a fixed order size and a varying order period. The system is that whenever the stock on hand falls to a certain minimal level, based on the time lag between order and delivery of the item, an order is automatically placed for the predetermined fixed amount. During the lead time period the order is already placed when the lead time period begins and any demand during this period may only be met from stock-on-hand. Therefore, there must be reserve stock to meet the fluctuations in demand during the lead time period. So it is determined by the two parameters: the reorder point and order quantity.

In Q-system inventory models involving uncertainty, it becomes apparent that the order quantity and reorder point are interdependent. The risk of stockout occurs only after the reorder point is reached. The size of the order quantity will determine how frequently the reorder point is reached. The larger the order quantity, the less frequent is the exposure to stockouts. In an annual period, if there is no more than one order outstanding at any given time, the number of time periods during which a stockout could occur is D/Q where D is the annual demand and Q is the order quantity. To account for the dependence between order quantities and reorder point, the expected annual cost formula for a continuous distribution with backordering is

Total expected annual cost = purchase cost + ordering cost + holding cost + stockout cost.

$$TC = DP + \frac{DO}{Q} + H\left[\frac{Q}{2} + \int_0^{\infty}(B - M)f(M)dM\right] + \frac{CD}{O}\int_B^{\infty}(M - B)f(M)dM$$

where, D is the average annual demand in units; P is the purchase cost per unit; O is the ordering cost per order; Q is the order quantity in units; H is the holding cost per unit per year; B is the reorder point in units; M is the lead time demand in units (a random variable); C is the stockout cost per unit; $f\,(M)$ is the probability density function of lead time demand.

The expected safety stock in units is expressed as

$$S = B - \overline{M} = \int_0^{\infty}(B - M)f(M)dM$$

Periodic Review Systems

Under the periodic review systems (P-system) of inventory control there is a fixed order period and a varying order size. The procedure is that at periodic intervals the amount of inventory level is reviewed and an order is placed. The total amount which should be on-hand and on-order is determined from the analysis so the amount of order is determined directly by subtracting the amount on hand from this predetermined total. The P-system is determined by the two parameters: the review period and the maximum inventory level. In the P-system the inventory position is monitored only at discrete points in time. Once an order is placed at time t, another order cannot be placed until $t + T$, and the second order will not be filled until the lead time period has elapsed, at time $t + t + L$. Thus, the safety stock protection is needed for the lead time L plus the order interval T.

7.2.2 Pharmaceutical Item Classification

To efficiently manage inventory of pharmaceutical items is to classify them and establish individual inventory policies for these classes. Thus, a standardized management of items within the same category, in terms of service levels, replenishment policies, etc. Traditional classification of inventory items includes ABC analysis based on annual consumption rate, VED classification based on item criticality and combination of both. The various factors considered by Danas et al. (2006) for classification of pharmaceuticals are patient treatment criticality, supply characteristics, inventory problems, and usage rate with the objective to make decisions on where to store safety stock in a hospital. The methodology used is multi-attribute tree analysis to classify the items into very important, important, less important and not important. To set the inventory control policies, Al-Qatawneh and Hafeez (2011) classified pharmaceutical items into three classes—high, medium, and low critical items based on factors, such as item criticality, usage, and cost of items. Other existing literature on classification of medical items include combination of ABC and VED classification (Kumar and Chakravarty 2015; Gupta et al. 2007). The limitation of these existing classifications is it is not always clear whether the item is critical or not as there is no quantitative technique used to measure the criticality of items. Gebicki et al. (2014) incorporated drug characteristics, such as drug criticality, availability, and expiration into inventory policy and evaluated the performance of several inventory policies in terms of drug and cost characteristics. The existing literature on classification of pharmaceuticals is listed in Table 7.1.

Table 7.1 Review of literature of classification of pharmaceuticals

Attributes	Decisions	Reference	Limitation
Patient treatment criticality, supply characteristics, inventory problems, usage rate	To make decisions on where to store safety stock	Danas et al. (2006)	Not always clear whether item is critical or not
Criticality, usage, cost	To set inventory control policies	Al-Qatawneh and Hafeez (2011)	
ABC-VED		Kumar and Chakravarty (2015), Gupta et al. (2007)	
Drug characteristics (criticality, availability, expiration)	To evaluate performance of inventory policies	Gebicki et al. (2014)	Classification not based on real settings, instead distributions were created

Pharmaceuticals are mainly the healthcare inventory items intended for the treatment, cure, prevention or diagnosis of diseases, abnormal physical states or symptoms, various health conditions of patient, etc. Mainly drug products dealt in healthcare settings, such as hospitals are the finished drug products purchased from the manufactures packed accordingly. Medicines are classified by World Health Organization, 2015 based on the needs for a basic healthcare system, listing the most efficacious, and safe and cost-effective medicines for priority conditions. Priority conditions are selected on the basis of current and estimated future public health relevance, and potential for safe and cost-effective treatment.

There are pharmaceuticals which cannot be delayed or omitted, such as all medicines used in emergency situations, anti-coagulants, anti-epileptics, anti-infectives, anti-parkinson medicines, insulin, steroids (oral and parenteral), and strong opioids prescribed regularly for acute or chronic pain.

The pharmaceuticals are classified at the various healthcare facilities based on number of factors, such as patient condition and diseases, consumption pattern, criticality of items, frequency of usage, price, availability, etc. The World Health Organization (WHO) Model List, 2015 classify the pharmaceuticals according to therapeutic categories for various medical conditions (McGuire 2011) as shown in Table 7.2.

The classification of pharmaceuticals may also be classified by WHO Model list, 2015 based on the dosage form as described in Table 7.3.

Table 7.2 WHO classification of pharmaceuticals based on therapeutic categories

Sl. No.	Pharmaceutical classes
1.	Anesthetics (general anesthetics and oxygen, local anesthetics, preoperative medication and sedation for short-term procedures)
2.	Medicines for pain and palliative care (non-opioids and non-steroidal anti-inflammatory medicines (NSAIMs), opioid analgesics, medicines for other common symptoms in palliative care)
3.	Antiallergics and medicines used in anaphylaxis
4.	Antidotes and other substances used in poisonings
5.	Anticonvulsants/antiepileptics
6.	Anti-infective medicines
7.	Antimigraine medicines
8.	Antineoplastics and immunosuppressives
9.	Antiparkinsonism medicines
10.	Medicines affecting the blood
11.	Cardiovascular medicines
12.	Dermatological medicines
13.	Diagnostic agents
14.	Diuretics
15.	Gastrointestinal medicines
16.	Hormones, other endocrine medicines and contraceptives
17.	Immunologicals
18.	Muscle relaxants (peripherally-acting) and cholinesterase inhibitors
19.	Ophthalmological preparations
20.	Oxytocics and antioxytocics
21.	Peritoneal dialysis solution
22.	Medicines for mental and behavioural disorders
23.	Medicines acting on the respiratory tract
24.	Solutions correcting water, electrolyte and acid–base disturbances
25.	Vitamins and minerals
26.	Ear, nose and throat medicines
27.	Specific medicines for neonatal care
28.	Medicines for diseases of joints

There are certain diseases which need either medication or surgical procedure at some point in time. According to the real data collected from a hospital, medicines are classified based on the patient condition. The classification based on the most commonly found patient diagnosis during the study period is shown in Table 7.4.

Table 7.3 WHO classification of pharmaceuticals based on dosage forms

Sl. No.	Dosage form	Description
1.	Solid ORAL (enteral)	Refers to tablets, capsules and granules
2.	Oral powder (enteral)	Preparations are issued to patient as powder to be taken in or with water or other suitable liquid
3.	Oral liquid (enteral)	Liquid preparations intended to be swallowed Includes drops, suspensions, emulsions, etc.
4.	Injection/intravenous infusion (parenteral)	Referred to solutions and emulsions constituted from powders or concentrated solutions
5.	Inhalation (parenteral)	Powders for inhalation, pressurized inhalation, nebulizer
6.	External	Includes lotion, gel, cream, ointment, spray, drops, etc.

Table 7.4 Classification of Pharmaceuticals based on patient condition

Sl. No.	Broad classification of patient condition
1.	Heart diseases (ischemic heart diseases, arrhythmia, cardiomyopathy)
2.	Hypertension
3.	Hypothyroidism
4.	Hepatitis A
5.	Hepatitis B
6.	Osteoporosis
7.	Abdominal pain
8.	Seizures
9.	Stroke
10.	Gastrointestinal disorders
11.	Gastroesophageal Reflux Disease (GERD)
12.	Diabetes (Type-1)
13.	Diabetes (Type-2)
14.	Diarrhea
15.	Chronic Obstructive Pulmonary Disease (COPD)
16.	Depression
17.	Constipation
18.	Cold and flu
19.	Cholesterol
20.	Bronchitis
21.	Asthma
22.	Arthritis (rheumatoid arthritis, osteoarthritis, gout)
23.	Attention deficit hyperactivity disorder (ADHD)
24.	Urinary tract infection
25.	Respiratory tract infection
26.	Acute intestinal obstruction

7.3 Demand Analysis of Pharmaceuticals at Healthcare Facilities

Analyzing demand of pharmaceuticals is the initial step in forecasting demand which is required for proper inventory management of pharmaceuticals. The requirement of pharmaceuticals in the healthcare facilities arises whenever the healthcare professionals prescribe pharmaceuticals for providing medical care and treatment to patients. The pharmaceuticals demand data comprises of list of all the orders requested by the pharmacy department to the external supplier with order date, items, and quantities for each pharmaceutical items. The pharmaceutical demand arises at multiple stages: patient-level where physician prescribe items for individual patient, hospital facility level where the items are stocked to meet the demand at patient-level and top-level, i.e., the hospital pharmacy which replenishes their stocks from the external suppliers to meet the demand at facility- and patient-level.

The pharmaceuticals demand may be aggregated with respect to time periods (daily, weekly, monthly, etc.), number of patients and groups of pharmaceutical items. The time-series demand data may be classified into time-series with pattern (linear—level, step, trend; nonlinear—periodic, cyclic; irregular—intermittent) and time-series with no pattern (erratic) as shown in Fig. 7.1.

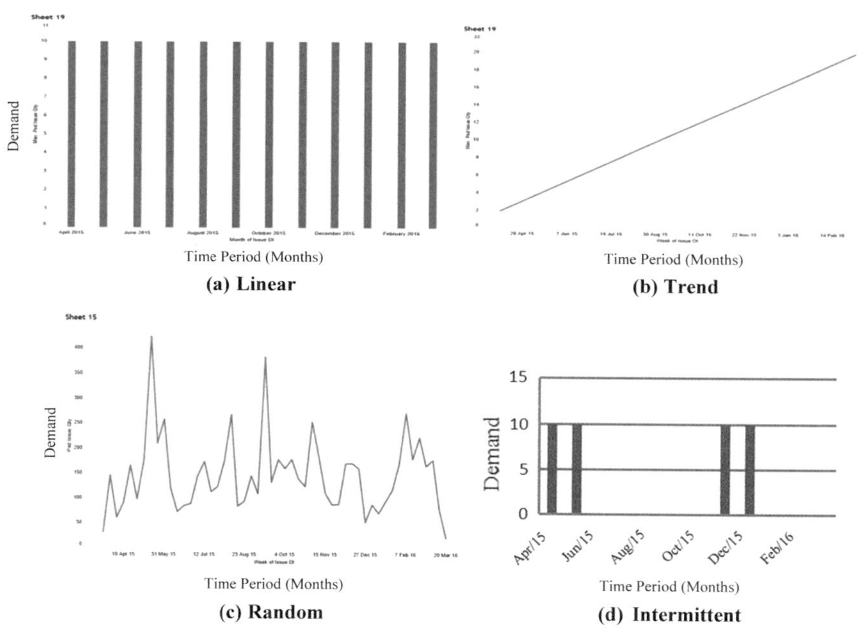

Fig. 7.1 a–d Time-series demand pattern of pharmaceutical items

The statistical distribution of individual demand as well as aggregate demand may be analyzed for understanding the demand variability and for demand forecasting. For static inventory problem, it is required to have knowledge of one demand probability distribution, i.e., the probability distribution of demand for the entire period to be covered by the inventory. However, in dynamic inventory problem, it is required to know the probability distribution of demand for varying length time intervals.

The demand distribution is modeled from two elements, i.e., the demand size and inter-demand interval. Thus, compound theoretical distributions that consider size-interval combination are used. In case time is considered a discrete variable, demand may be generated based on a Bernoulli process, resulting in geometric distribution of inter-demand intervals and when the time is considered as continuous variable, the poisson demand generation process results in negative exponentially distributed inter-arrival intervals (Syntetos and Boylan 2011).

7.4 Inventory Control of Pharmaceuticals at Healthcare Facilities

The purpose of inventory control at the facility level is to (i) prepare effective orders, (ii) maintain sufficient safety stocks, (iii) adjust inventory levels to respond to changes in patient condition, treatment procedures, etc., (iv) provide appropriate, safe and secure storage, and (v) prevent expiry of medicines. The ultimate goal of inventory control is to ensure that the right medicines are kept in the right quantities and are available at the right time. The benefits of a successful inventory control system at the facility level are (i) prompt administration of medicines to patients, (ii) prevention of stockouts even when deliveries are delayed, and (iii) proper patient care. The problems arising from poor inventory control are (i) a patient's condition may worsen or antimicrobial resistance may develop because of a delay in treatment or a patient may even die if a lifesaving medicine is out of stock, (ii) emergency orders, which are expensive for the purchaser and inconvenient for the suppliers, may be required. The following subsections describes the various elements, parameters, and factors involved in pharmaceutical inventory control systems.

7.4.1 Elements of Pharmaceutical Inventory Control Systems

The elements of pharmaceutical inventory control systems includes stock list of pharmaceuticals, current stock-on-hand, stock-on-order, net stock, inventory position, expected replenishment lead time, remaining shelf-life, inventory-related costs (ordering costs, holding costs, stockout costs, emergency order cost).

7.4.2 Pharmaceutical Inventory Control Systems and Parameters

The inventory control systems for pharmaceutical items are periodic review systems, continuous review systems, and combination systems. In case of perfectly predictable demand without any variability, a fixed-order quantity may be ordered at every review, but as the demand is variable either variable quantities are ordered at fixed review periods, i.e., periodic review systems or fixed quantities are ordered at variable intervals, i.e., continuous review systems.

The various inventory control parameters are the order quantity and reorder level for continuous review inventory policy; review period and maximum inventory level for the periodic inventory policy and maximum and minimum par level for the order-up-to level policy.

7.4.3 Factors Involved in Pharmaceutical Inventory Management

The various factors involved in pharmaceutical inventory management are the patient characteristics which include number of patients arriving, transferring and discharging, their changing health condition during their length-of-stay in hospitals, etc., the characteristics of pharmaceutical products which include price of items, criticality, availability and expiration of items, patient-level and item-level demand pattern and its distribution and lead time variability.

The criticality may be patient-oriented, product-oriented, and area-oriented. The patient-oriented criticality is defined based on the danger of loss of life, quality of treatment, and replacement with other treatments (Danas et al. 2006). In the product-oriented criticality, some items individually may not be critical, but may be critical for the completion of the treatment procedure. The criticality of the patient also depends on the area where the patient is admitted or treated, i.e., emergency room, critical care unit, high dependency unit, operation room, ward, etc.

7.5 Study Methodology

The system under consideration is stochastic due to the change in number of patients arriving and discharging with time, changes in patient condition with time during their stay in hospital, transfer from one hospital bed to another also changes with time during their stay in hospital, and thus the demand size of items also changes with time. The methodology adopted for analyzing the performance of an inventory system includes the preliminary study, data collection and analysis, classification of pharmaceutical items, and inventory control models and is described in following steps:

Step 1: Preliminary Study

Initially, the various operations and processes of the system are observed thoroughly. Discussion with the hospital managers and staff provides preliminary information regarding the present scenario of the hospital, hospital administration, problems faced by the patients and/or medical personnel related to inventory system, certain constraints at the tactical, strategic and operation level, factors affecting the inventory system, etc. This leads to overall study plan which includes the decision regarding type of data to be collected, the methods and the duration of data collection and the improvement alternative inventory policy to be evaluated in order to address the specific problems faced by the system under consideration.

Step 2: Data Collection and Analysis

The patient information and medicine information is collected from the hospital information management systems. The patient-related information data included patient ID and name, date of arrival and discharge, provisional and final diagnosis, physician allotted and specialty. The medicine-related information includes patient ID and name, medicines issued, date of issuance, quantity issued, and unit price. The structure of the data is shown in Table 7.5.

The descriptive statistics of the data collected are shown in Table 7.6.

The patient arrival pattern and distribution and the distribution of length-of-stay of patients in hospital are analyzed and shown in Fig. 7.2a–d.

The demand of a pharmaceutical item (solutions correcting water, electrolyte and acid–base disturbances) in various specialties in a hospital, such as cardiology, neurology, and others is shown in Fig. 7.3.

Step 3: Classification of Pharmaceutical Items

The pharmaceutical products are classified based on (i) patient condition which includes severity of illness of patient admitted in a hospital, type of specialty and timeliness of administration of items, (ii) demand characteristics and (iii) unit price of items.

The statistical information for issuance of pharmaceutical items is available for one financial year (April 2015 to March 2016). The demand information is recorded in daily time periods, so a total of 366 periods of demand information is available for the study. The pharmaceutical items include two main categories—items related to patient condition and items not related to any particular patient condition. There are total 5364 pharmaceutical items recorded in the hospital from where the data is collected. The items related to the patient condition are classified according to criticality as follows:

Table 7.5 Structure of the data collected

Patient profile					Medicine profile (type* and demand)				
Patient ID	Date of arrival	Length-of-stay	Specialty	Diagnosis	Type-1	…	Type-6	…	Type-28
IP/15/01988	01/04/2015	11	CARD	Angina	0	…	13	…	0

*Refer to Table 7.2

Table 7.6 Descriptive statistics of the data collected

	Total number	Mean	Range	Variable type
Number of patients	4057	–	–	–
Length-of-stay	–	16.97	1–79	Numeric
Specialty	21	–	1–21	String (1—cardiology, … 21—urology)
Diagnosis**	1–26	–	1–26	String (1—heart disease … 26—acute intestinal obstruction)
Medicine type	1–28	–	1–28	String (1—anesthetics … 28—medicines for diseases of joints)
Quantity demanded	–	26.07	1–200	Numeric
Unit price	–	703.59	0.21–75,000	Numeric

**Refer to Table 7.4

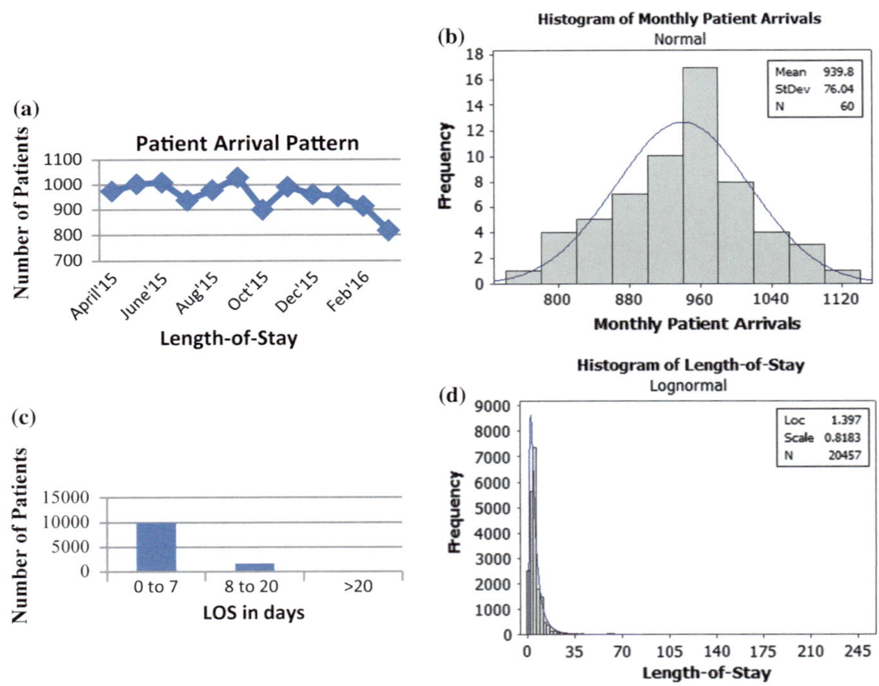

Fig. 7.2 a–d Patient arrival and length-of-stay pattern and distribution

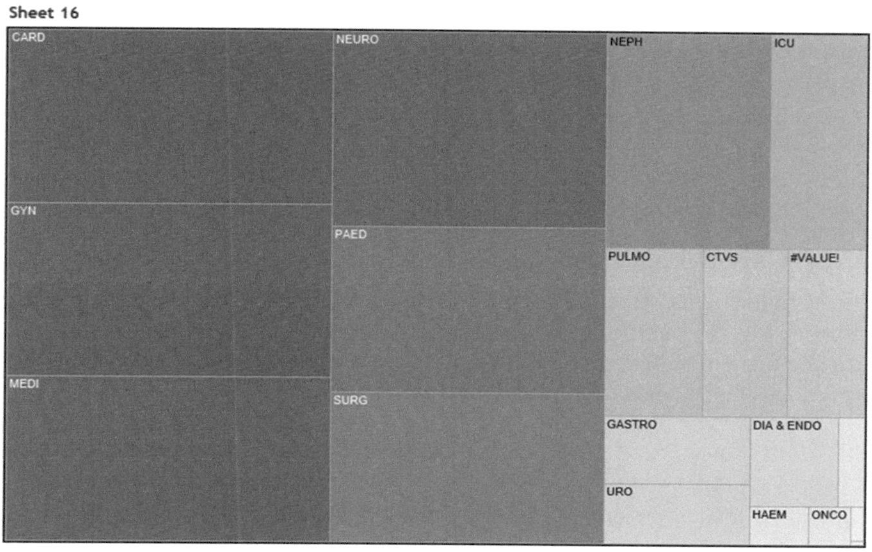

Fig. 7.3 Demand of a pharmaceutical item

(i) Highly Critical (HC): Unavailability of these items would result in danger to the life of patient.
(ii) Moderately Critical (MC): Unavailability of these items does not endanger the life of patient but are significant for the treatment and care of the patient.
(iii) Less Critical (LC): Unavailability of these items would not result in serious effects on the treatment and life of the patient.

No quantitative method is used for this classification. A further inspection of items with criticality leads to a more refined classification based on combined criticality, i.e., HC/MC/LC, MC/LC depending on the requirement of the items to multiple patient condition of different criticality. Based on the criticality the stock levels are decided—items identified as highly critical are kept on stock as they require high fill rates, moderately critical items are kept on stock depending on the cost-effective consideration, and low critical ones destock. A more refined analysis of pharmaceutical items data revealed that important differences among them existed not only in terms of criticality but also with respect to demand and price. Therefore, it is aimed at grouping them in different classes to see whether it is required to apply different stock control methods for different classes (Porras and Dekker 2008). Thus, the different classes considered are based on patient condition, demand and price of items are described below.

(a) Patient Condition Classes

The classification based on patient condition is to achieve clinical homogeneity in regard of the utilization of resources. The factors that influence the amount of resources are the complications in patient condition, co-morbidities present in the patient and treatment type, i.e., whether surgery or medication. Based on the timeliness of administration of items there are certain time-critical scheduled items like insulin, etc., and there are certain non-time-critical scheduled items. The factors defining patient condition are patient criticality, types of beds, and length of stay. Thus, the patient condition is measured by considering complications, co-morbidities, treatment and test procedures, type of bed and length-of-stay.

Complications

Complications which may develop on the patients during the treatment and may influence the amount of resources/medications used to treat the patient. For example, patient suffering chronic kidney disease with left ventricular failure will likely incur higher medication than a member without left ventricular failure.

Co-morbidities

A patient's prior medical history may impact the type and quantity of resources required to treat a patient. As in the example of patient suffering from chronic kidney disease with left ventricular failure, a patient with a history of hypertension and/or diabetes mellitus requires more resources than a patient without those conditions. The feature of classification specifically differentiates chronic kidney disease with complication with co-morbidity from chronic kidney disease without complication without co-morbidity.

Treatment and Tests Procedures

The classification differs in resource consumptions among patients with different treatment and test procedures. The treatment and tests procedures include surgery, medication, diagnostic, and laboratory tests.

Types of Bed

The type of bed occupied by the patient depends on the patients' medical condition. There are several types of bed occupied by patient during their stay in the hospital. Based on the types of bed occupied by the patient the daily rate of consumption of medications depends. For example, intensive care unit patients may require more quantity of certain drug in a day than the patient in wards.

Length-of-Stay

The total length-of-stay of patients' admitted in the hospital depends on the medical condition of the patient. More critical patient tends to stay for a longer period of time in the hospital than less critical patient and consequently, the rate of consumption of resources are more for long-stay patients.

(b) Demand Classes

The original data set consisted of 5364 pharmaceutical items, for which high variability in demand patterns is observed. For example, some items have only 0/1 demands while others experienced either large demands or no demands for few months. Thus, a classification is required for the items based on the consumption rates. The boundary between groups was not clearly identified in histogram of demand but from Pareto Analysis it could reasonably establish in 250 units.

According to the histogram of demand and Pareto Analysis, the following demand classes for the items are identified as shown in Table 7.7.

Demand Class-1: Items with only 0/1 demand
Demand Class-2: Items with total demand larger than 1 but less than 250 units
Demand Class-3: Items with total demand higher than 250 units

The classification of demand pattern is as shown in Fig. 7.4. Four quadrants are determined based on two dimensions: demand size variability (measured by CV^2) and average demand inter-arrival interval (measured by ADI), considering cutoff values of 0.49 and 1.32 respectively from the literature (do Rego and de Mesquita 2015; Nenes et al. 2010).

The possible factors contributing to the intermittence in the demand pattern may be numerous patient admission and frequency of patient and physician demand, and the possible factors contributing to the erratic behavior in the demand pattern may be heterogeneity of patient and their condition and variety of patient and physician demands which may be measured by coefficient of variation of demand of a single patient.

(c) Price Classes

For the pharmaceutical items in the data set, five different price levels were identified in a histogram. Table 7.8 shows the different price classes for the pharmaceutical items. It is observed that prices were low as Rs. 0.23 and most expensive item price as Rs. 75,000.

Table 7.7 Demand classes

Demand class	1	2	3
Demand (d) in units	$d = 0, 1$	$1 < d \leq 250$	$d > 250$
Items (total = 5364)	448 (8.35%)	3992 (74.4%)	924 (17.2%)

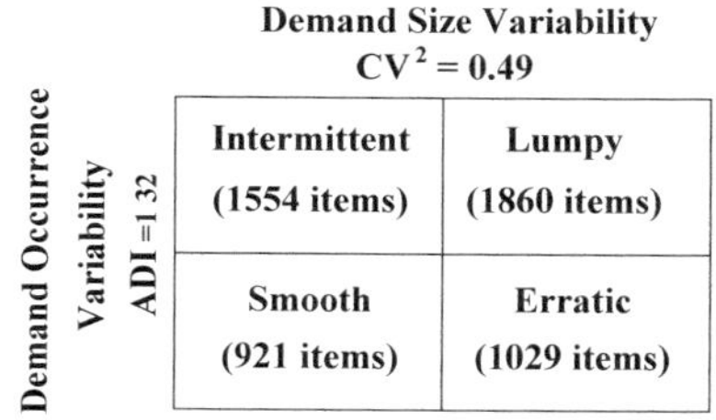

Fig. 7.4 Demand classification of pharmaceutical items

Table 7.8 Price classes

Price class	1	2	3	4	5
Price (p) in Rs.	$0 < p \leq 73.3$	$73.3 < p \leq 146.6$	$146.6 < p \leq 219.9$	$219.9 < p \leq 293.2$	$p > 293.2$
Items (total = 5364)	3548 (66.14%)	565 (10.53%)	224 (4.17%)	172 (3.20%)	855 (15.93%)

(d) Combined Classes

Using criticality, demand and price classes, we include each item in a combined class defined by three digits 'xyz'. Accordingly, an item in class 'xyz' corresponds to an item with demand class x, criticality class y and price class z. this classification allows us to optimize the system per class rather than for individual items. That is, once a service level is defined for he combined class, the parameters for the different inventory policies are evaluated for each item in the class.

Step 4: Inventory Control Models

The inventory control models depend on the type of demand pattern followed by the pharmaceutical items, such as inventory models with intermittent, erratic and lumpy demand.

Inventory Models with Intermittent Demand

The distinguishing feature in the model of controlling inventories with intermittent demands is the use of probability distribution with a spike at zero to represent the relative frequency of periods with no transactions (Engelmeyer 2016). Thus, the assumption of normal distribution may lead to poor results. Intermittent demand series have a low mean value and a relatively high variance. Therefore, a normal distribution based on those values will have a considerable positive density in the negative range. To avoid these problems, the literature provides inventory policies which are based on the gamma distribution which is only defined for positive values, Poisson distribution and negative binomial distributions of demand (Snyder et al. 2012). Once forecasts of demand are obtained, they are fed into the inventory control decision process and may be solved by simulation.

Inventory Models with Erratic Demand

Erratic demand is characterized by irregular demand sizes with high variations. Erratic demands have traditionally shown complexities in inventory management. Combination of distributions are recommended in the literature to model erratic demand distributions, such as combination of poisson and geometric distribution (sluttering Poisson), poisson and logarithmic distribution (negative binomial distribution), Bernoulli and logarithmic-poisson distribution (compound poisson) for demand occurrences and demand sizes, respectively. In case of continuous demand, gamma distribution may be approximated as the distribution of demand. In case of continuous demand data triangular and beta distributions are found to be applicable for modeling erratic demand (Onyeocha et al. 2014).

Inventory Models with Lumpy Demands

A lumpy demand pattern is characterized by large transactions separated by periods of zero demand. The problem of controlling items with lumpy demand patterns has received considerable less attention although these items constitute an appreciable portion of the inventory items. A compound poisson distribution is generally suggested in the existing literature to approximate the nature of the demand and a continuous review policy is used to control the inventory systems (Mak et al. 1999). Schultz (1987) considered a base-stock inventory policy with periodic review for lumpy demand pattern.

For example, a pharmaceutical item with Item ID BRI088Z and Item Name BRILINTA 90 MG TAB to treat patient with heart disease, demand class is 3 and demand pattern 'Erratic' and price class 1 is considered with demand characteristics as shown in Figs. 7.5, 7.6, and 7.7.

Three types of costs are associated with inventories—holding cost, ordering costs, and stockout costs. Holding cost represents the cost of capital tied up in the pharmaceutical items inventory. An annual fixed rate of 11% was used in the study. Ordering cost represent the cost associated with placing an order, which includes the costs of telephone calls/system indent preparation, inspection and handling of incoming items, etc., this cost is independent of number of items included in the order. An ordering cost of Rs 10 per order is used for the study. In case of stockout, emergency order is placed and immediately the item is replenished. The emergency ordering cost is higher than the regular ordering cost.

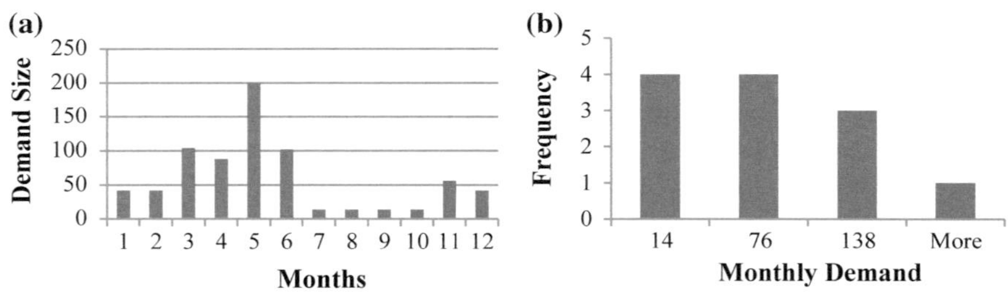

Fig. 7.5 **a**, **b** Time series and histogram of monthly demand of Item ID BRI088Z in the year 2015–2016

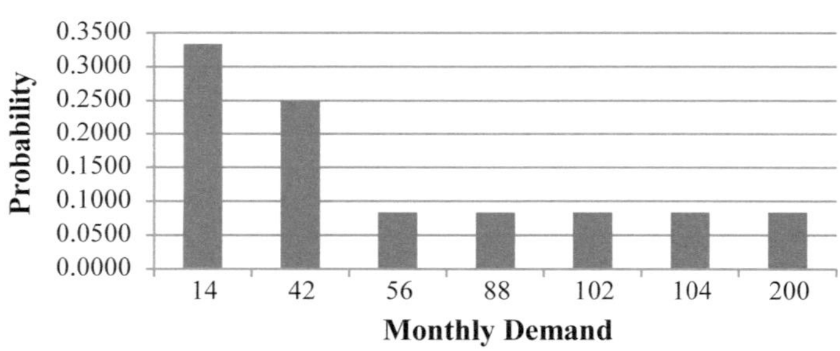

Fig. 7.6 Probability distribution of monthly demand of Item ID BRI088Z in the year 2015–2016

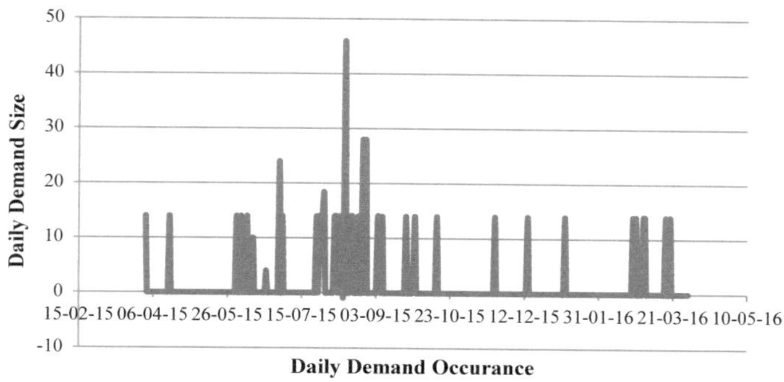

Fig. 7.7 Daily demand occurrence vs daily demand size of Item ID BRI088Z in the year 2015–2016

7.6 Concluding Remarks

Pharmaceutical items, particularly those subject to rare critical diseases and patient condition, possess considerable challenge for both demand planning and inventory management. If inventory decisions are not proper, then the result may lead to poor patient service or excessive stock, possibly leading to expiration, and in the other hand, effective demand modeling and inventory control may lead to cost savings and improved patient service. Classification of pharmaceutical items is an essential element in their inventory management that serve several purposes, such as determination of target service level, establishment of inventory decisions, choice of demand forecasting approach and method. Determining service level requirements is achieved by patient condition criticality classification and by assessing the severity of illness of patient by the factors like complications and co-morbidities in patients. A further aim of classification is to determine the demand modeling method by analyzing the various pharmaceutical items with intermittent and erratic demand pattern and accordingly inventory of those items are managed. The analysis of patient demand pattern are relevant for understanding the variability as well as for forecasts and their accuracy and it also allows monitoring consistent use of inventory policies. For further study empirical evidence in this field is required to be explored.

References

Al-Qatawneh, L., & Hafeez, K. (2011). Healthcare logistics cost optimization using a multi-criteria inventory classification. International Conference on Industrial Engineering and Operations Management, Kuala Lumpur.

Attanayake, N., Kashef, R., & Andrea, T. (2014). A Simulation model for a continuous review inventory policy for healthcare system. In: 27th Canadian Conference on Electrical and Computer Engineering (CCECE). IEEE, pp. 1–6.

Danas, K., Roudsari, A., & Ketikidis, P. H. (2006). The applicability of a multi-attribute classification framework in the healthcare industry. *Journal of Manufacturing Technology Management, 17,* 772–785.
de Vries, J. (2011). The shaping of inventory systems in health services: A stakeholder analysis. *International Journal of Production Economics, 133,* 60–69.
do Rego, J. R., & de Mesquita, M. A. (2015). Demand forecasting and inventory control: A simulation study on automotive spare parts. *International Journal of Production Economics, 161,* 1–16.
Engelmeyer, T. (2016). Managing intermittent demand. Wiesbaden: Springer Fachmedien Wiesbaden.
Gebicki, M., Mooney, E., Chen, S.-J.G., & Mazur, L. M. (2014). Evaluation of hospital medication inventory policies. *Health Care Management Science, 17,* 215–229.
Guerrero, W., Yeung, T., & Guéret, C. (2013). Joint-optimization of inventory policies on a multi-product multi-echelon pharmaceutical system with batching and ordering constraints. *European Journal of Operational Research, 231*(1), 98–108.
Gupta, R., Gupta, K. K., Jain, B. R., & Garg, R. (2007). ABC and VED analysis in medical stores inventory control. *Medical Journal Armed Forces India, 63,* 325–327.
Kelle, P., Woosley, J., & Schneider, H. (2012). Pharmaceutical supply chain specifics and inventory solutions for a hospital case. *Operations Research for Health Care, 1*(2–3), 54–63.
Kumar, S., & Chakravarty, A. (2015). ABC–VED analysis of expendable medical stores at a tertiary care hospital. *Medical Journal Armed Forces India, 71*(1), 24–27.
Little, J., & Coughlan, B. (2008). Optimal inventory policy within hospital space constraints. *Health Care Management Science, 11*(2), 177–183.
Mak, K. L., Wong, Y. S., & Huang, G. Q. (1999). Optimal inventory control of lumpy demand items using genetic algorithms. *Computers & Industrial Engineering, 37,* 273–276.
McGuire, G. (2011). *Handbook of humanitarian healthcare logistics: Designing the supply network and managing the flows of information and health care goods in humanitarian assistance during complex political emergencies* (2nd ed.), www.humanitarianhealthcarelo-gistics.com
Nenes, G., Panagiotidou, S., & Tagaras, G. (2010). Invenory management of multiple items with irregular demand: A case study. *European Journal of Operational Research, 205,* 313–324.
Nicholson, L., Vakharia, A., & Erenguc, S. S. (2004). Outsourcing inventory management decisions in healthcare: Models and application. *European Journal of Operational Research, 154*(1), 271–290.
Onyeocha, C. E., Khoury, J., & Harik, R. F. (2014). Evaluation of forecasting and inventory control in multi-product manufacturing systems operating under erratic demand: A case study in the automotive domain. *Computer Science and Applications, 1*(1), 31–47.
Porras, E., & Rommert, R. (2008). An inventory control system for spare parts at a refinery: An empirical comparison of different re-order point methods. *European Journal of Operational Research, 184,* 101–132.
Roni, M., Jin, M., & Eksioglu, S. (2015). A hybrid inventory management system responding to regular demand and surge demand. *Omega, 52,* 190–200.
Saha, E., & Ray, P. K. (2016). An overview of impact of healthcare inventory management systems on entrepreneurship. In Eds. P. Mandal & J. Vong (Eds.), *Entrepreneurship in technology for ASEAN: Part of the series managing the Asian century* (pp. 83–94). Berlin: Springer.
Şatir, A., & Cengiz, D. (1987). Medicinal inventory control in a university health centre. *Journal of the Operational Research Society, 38*(5), 387–395.
Schultz, C. R. (1987). Forecasting and inventory control for sporadic demand under periodic review. *Journal of the Operational Research Society, 38.*
Snyder, R. D., Ord, J. K., & Beaumont, A. (2012). Forecasting the intermittent demand for slow-moving inventories: A modelling approach. *International Journal of Forecasting, 28,* 485–496.

Syntetos, A. A., & Boylan, J. E. (2011). Intermittent demand: Estimation and statistical properties. In N. Altay & L.A. Litteral (Eds.), *Service parts management, demand forecasting and inventory control.* Berlin: Springer.

Uthayakumar, R., & Priyan, S. (2013). Pharmaceutical supply chain and inventory management strategies: Optimization for a pharmaceutical company and a hospital. *Operations Research for Health Care, 2*(3), 52–64.

Vila-Parrish, A. R., Ivy, J. S., King, R. E., & Abel, S. R. (2012). Patient-based pharmaceutical inventory management: A two-stage inventory and production model for perishable products with Markovian demand. *Health Systems, 1,* 69–83.

Chapter 8
A Comprehensive Framework for Ergonomic Evaluation of Patient Handling Jobs in Healthcare Systems

Sanjeet Kumar and Pradip Kumar Ray

Abstract In recent times, it is essential, for any products or systems, to apply ergonomic principles in their human–machine interactions for enhancement of system performance with negligible or very less negative effect of human work on human health. The workers in hospitals, loading and unloading the stretchers with patients into an ambulance, may face a number of health-related problems like musculoskeletal disorders, back injuries, etc. For eliminating these types of problems, researchers and practitioners have proposed several approaches addressed by the difficulties and health disorder faced by the workers to study on ergonomic improvement of patient transfer to the ambulance and other places. We need to critically appraise these approaches. In this paper, the details of these approaches being recommended for healthcare service delivery system have been discussed and critically appraised.

Keywords Human–machine interaction · Ergonomic application · Musculoskeletal disorder · Patient handling · Appraisal of existing approaches

8.1 Introduction

The caregivers and nursing staff working in hospitals, many a time, use to do manual lifting, transferring, repositioning, and moving the patients from one place to another. These types of jobs performed by the nursing staff are referred to as patient handling jobs. In any healthcare systems patient handling jobs are considered one of the most critical jobs for nursing staff. The nursing staff usually may face different types of health problems and injuries while performing patient han-

S. Kumar (✉) · P.K. Ray
Department of Industrial and Systems Engineering,
Indian Institute of Technology Kharagpur, Kharagpur, India
e-mail: sanjeet.mgz@gmail.com

P.K. Ray
e-mail: pkr@vgsom.iitkgp.ernet.in

P.K. Ray and J. Maiti (eds.), *Healthcare Systems Management: Methodologies and Applications*, Managing the Asian Century,
DOI 10.1007/978-981-10-5631-4_8

dling jobs. As has been reported by researchers, one of the most common injuries occurring in nursing staff due to patient handling jobs is musculoskeletal disorders (MSDs). Among the nursing staff pains in different body parts such as back, knee, and neck are also very common injuries with consequences like increased absenteeism and adverse effect on health.

8.1.1 Various Types of Patient Handling Jobs

A set of typical patient handling jobs carried out in the healthcare systems are as follows:

i. Transfer the patients on stretcher from one place to another,
ii. Moving the patients from stretcher to bed and vice versa,
iii. Repositioning the patients on the bed,
iv. Moving the patients from wheelchair to toilet and vice versa, and
v. Transfer the patient through wheelchair.

A patient handling job can be done by using one or more patient handling devices. To make the patient handling devices safe and comfortable to use by the nursing personnel, the design of human–machine interaction should be improved. It is desired that any such jobs are assessed with respect to quality of human–machine interaction or interface.

Some of the patient handling jobs (Skotte et al. 2002) are illustrated in Figs. 8.1, 8.2, 8.3, 8.4, 8.5, 8.6, 8.7, 8.8, 8.9, and 8.10.

Fig. 8.1 Standard lifting job

Fig. 8.2 Lifting the patient from sitting on the edge of the bed to standing on the floor

Fig. 8.3 Repositioning of the supine patient toward the head of the bed

Fig. 8.4 Elevate the patient from a supine position in the bed to sitting position on the edge of the bed

Fig. 8.5 Repositioning the patient posteriorly in the seat of the wheelchair

8.1.2 Ergonomic Problems Related to Patient Handling Jobs

As has been found through research, the process of loading a stretcher into an ambulance is known to cause a high incidence of back injuries among paramedic

Fig. 8.6 Turning the patient in bed away from nursing staff from his back to side

Fig. 8.7 Transferring the patient from sitting on the bed to sitting in a wheelchair

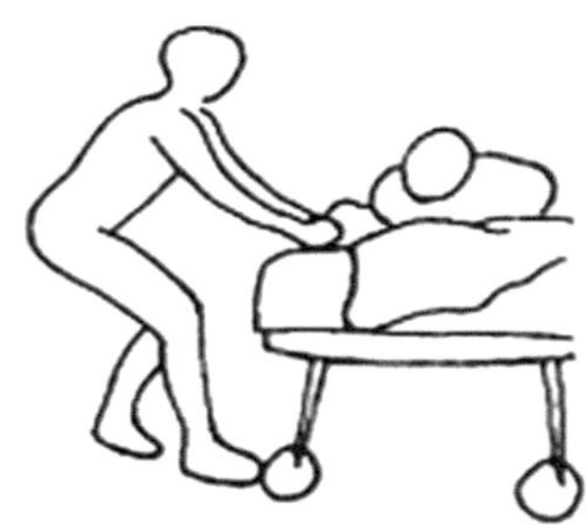

Fig. 8.8 Repositioning of the patient from lying in the middle of the bed to the bedside nearest the nursing staff

(Prairie et al. 2016). Holstrom et al. (1993) conclude that 92% of the workers had experienced musculoskeletal symptoms like localized pain or discomfort; the most prevalent symptoms were located in the back (72%), Knees (52%), neck (37%), and right shoulder (37%) for such a job. Lifting of patients is considered to be the heaviest task by about 73% of the nursing aids and bed-making in a stooping poster by 21% (Garg and Owen 1994). Research into manual handling suggests that the most probable failure mode for low back injury results from compression of the L4/S1 intervertebral disk (Prairie et al. 2016). The movement of trunk and flexion in

Fig. 8.9 Moving the patient from sitting on the bed to supine position in the bed

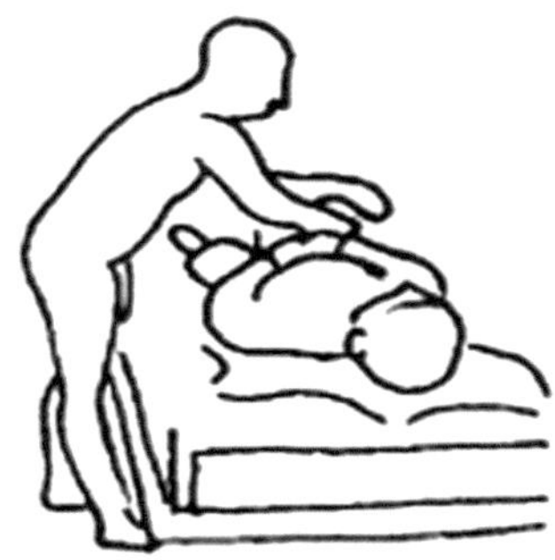

Fig. 8.10 Turning the patient in bed toward the nursing staff from his back to his left side

spine causes low back disordered among the nursing staff while performing the wound-dressing task (Szeto et al. 2013). Le Bon and Forrester (1997) evaluate the use of patient handling devices called elevate and transfer vehicle and found that the nurses may have a negative attitude toward patient handling devices. Owen (1988) reported that the use of patient handling devices may be underutilized because of a number of reasons: Increased time to perform the transfer (Owen et al. 1992; Garg and Owen 1994), unsafe condition while performing the work with devices (Owen et al. 1992), physical stress to nursing staff (Warming et al. 2009; Barrett and Dennis 2005; Elford et al. 2000), and preference of Patient and Nursing staff to do manual handling (Barrett and Dennis 2005; Waaijer 2014; Hignett and Richardson 1997).

8.1.3 Objectives and Scope of Research

The main objective of the study is to analyze different types of problems being encountered by the nursing staff for patient handling jobs working in hospitals and to suggest possible improvements in the design of such jobs. It is expected that through such improvements in place, nursing staff can do their assigned jobs with ease and minimum risk of injuries and patient feel comfortable.

8.2 Review of Literature

Loading and unloading stretchers to ambulance cause back injuries by paramedics. A study has been done on Biomechanical risk assessment during field loading of hydraulic stretchers into ambulances (Prairie et al. 2016). In their study they have observed 58 paramedics who are engaged 258 stretcher loading operations performed over 311 emergency calls during consistent 8 or 12 hours day (n = 34 paramedics) and night (n = 24 paramedics) work shift and data were collected for 111 days. With the help of 3DSSP program and data collected they have estimated the compression and shear forces at L5/S1. They have done multiple regression analysis for compression force (considering the variables Hand Load, Back Sagittal Flexion and elbow angle) and shear force (considering the variable Hand Load, Back Sagittal Flexion and Weight of the paramedics). Out of 258 stretcher loading activities they have analyzed 171 loading activities by regression model and they found that the compressive criterion limits are exceeded in 71% of cases and none has exceeded the shear criterion limits.

By using one or two caregivers for patient transfer, a biomechanical assessment of flour and overhead lifts has been done (Dutta et al. 2012). They have considered as protocol of their study in which the estimation of compression at the L5/S1 joint was found by a single equivalent muscle model which did not account for coactivity of antagonistic muscles and improved study by collecting ground reaction forces using newly developed force shoe rather than force plate to allow the caregivers to move more naturally. In this paper author used an EMG-assisted model for their study and estimated the hand force and external moment at L5/S1 from ground reaction force and data collected through questionnaire for the patient handling job from a wheelchair to bed and bed to wheelchair using floor and overhead lifts in a simulated clinical environment and the result shows that the force required by overhead lift was lower than the floor lift. Also they have studied the patient handling job using two caregivers and they found that in the case of the floor lift the load on primary caregivers did not reduce compared to single caregiver–patient handling, but in the case of overhead lift, the load was reduced on caregivers using two caregivers compared to single caregivers.

A dynamic 3D biomechanical evaluation of the load on the low back during different patient handling tasks (Skotte et al. 2002) has been done in which they have classified the patient handling tasks in three groups: Lifting, Repositioning, and Turning. In their study they have considered 10 female healthcare workers having job experience of 19 (6–26) years, and currently they are handling the job of 7 (2–20) patients per day without any special training considering patient handling techniques. In this study 3D biomechanical model has been used for the calculation of net torque at the L4/L5 joint. Force plate has been used for calculation of ground reaction and force transducer is fitted in bed for bedside reaction. EMG is used for measurement of muscles activity, with the help of 50 Hz video system using five cameras, and total experiment has been captured and digitalized automatically with the help of Peak Motus 4.3 system. After completion of patient handling task healthcare workers have been asked to rate her Perceived Physical Exertion (RPE) on the low back using Borg Scale (0 means nothing at all and 10 means exertion were extremely strong). The results show that compression force and shear force were high task dependent whereas EMG data and RPE are values dependent on subjects. The peak value of compression of two task involving lifting (4132/4433 N) was higher than all other tasks: four tasks involving repositioning the patient in the bed (3179/3091/2931/3094) and two tasks involving turning (1618/2197 N).

Effect of multi-component patient handling intervention which upgrade the attitude and behavior of nursing staff toward the safe patient handling and also reduces the aggression experienced by the nursing staff (Risor et al. 2017). They have evaluated the use of patient handling equipment by the nursing staff for the intervention and controlled group, questionnaires were made through the data collected from both the groups before the intervention and after 12 month from the intervention. After the analysis of questionnaires made from these data, authors concluded that the intervention groups have more positive approach toward the use of patient handling equipment as compared to controlled group nursing staff and also the intervention group nursing staff experienced less physically aggressive episode compared to the controlled group nursing staff; however, there were not significant change in health and days of absence on the nursing staff during this period.

A study on “Risk assessment of patient handling with ambulance stretcher systems (ramp/winch), easy-loader, tail-lift using biomechanical failure” has been done (Cooper and Ghassemieh 2007) in which they have considered 12 ambulance workers having an equal number of men and women. The means and standard deviations of their ages were 37 ± 4 years, their weights were 73 ± 6 kg, and heights were 1.8 ± 0.1 m. The forces exerted by the workers on the ambulance have attached with the stretcher frame. The force handle was attached with the been measured by the force handle load cell which produced voltage according to applied force. By measuring the voltage they have determined the forces using calibration. The loading and unloading processes were video recorded by a high-quality camera and biomechanical analyses of different stages of postures have been done using 3DSSPP developed by Michigan University. They had synchronized the forces measured by the load cell and video footage. They have also done kinetic analyses for all the loading systems considering different postures, and exerted forces on the stretcher were calculated using the failure criterion limit for different working postures set by the Snook et al. BS EN 1005-3 and BSEN 1865. They have found that the measured forces by the load cell very much agreed by the estimated forces using kinetic analyses. After analyses they have found some critical position, such as easy-loader system and ramp system. Easy-load system requires load which exceed safe limit and hence it is not advised, whereas, ramp system appeared safe for the patient with weight of around 75 kg, but in case the limit exceeds this limit, it is advised to use ramp system without winch and with good training of ambulance workers so that they can share the load properly to avoid injuries.

A study on "Biomechanical analysis of two patient handling tasks" has been done (Lindbeck and Engkvist 1993) and in their study they have tried to analyze the patient handling task semi-dynamically because the fully dynamic analysis of patients handling seems complicated to carry out and require sophisticated and expensive equipment. Semi-dynamically analysis is the analysis in which the segmental contribution of the whole body acceleration is ignored. They have considered two patient handling tasks: first "turning patient on bed" and second "moving the patient up the bed". They have considered 12 physiotherapists as subjects and two patients were engaged at a time for moving the patient using draws sheet and friction reducing plastic sheets. In this study they have assumed that the hand force and direction applied by the hand load were known. They have used the force plate and selspot to measure the moments about the L5/S1. Free body diagram is used for the part below: L5/S1 and 2DSSPP models were used for the top segment of body. The result of this study says that there were no requirements of fully dynamic analysis of the task as the segmental contributions to the inertial effects were negligible.

A study on "biomechanical evaluation of patient handling jobs in healthcare: a case study in India" has been done (Ray and Saha 2017) in which dynamic biomechanical model has been used for the patient handling task such as lifting patients from beds to stretchers, placing them on wheelchair or giving support through shoulders during physical diagnosis. They have calculated all the relevant forces and acceleration (linear and angular) using kinetic analysis and Ariel Performance Analysis System (APAS), respectively. The result showed that the moment along the hand, Lower arm, upper arm, and trunk segment were the higher than the threshold value and most critical joints were the wrist and shoulder.

A comparison of the risk of injury to the lumbar spine in the patient handling using slings and not using slings has been done (Elford et al. 2000) in which three patient handling techniques used in healthcare system for carrying a patient from one chair to another chair involving two subjects (1) without sling, (2) with one sling, and (3) with two slings. They have used kinematic variables and subjective ratings of body part stresses and preference of the lifting techniques in their study of twenty-two nurses performed five times in each of the three techniques used. Their results show that angular displacement, velocity, and acceleration were significantly greater in the frontal, sagittal, and transverse planes for the no sling technique compared to others. Using no sling technique there were higher mean total body stress and the first preference for the nurses who were using the techniques with a sling. There was a higher risk of injury and stresses in no sling technique compared to all others.

It is a study on designing ergonomic intervention for emergency medical services (EMS) workers having musculoskeletal injuries due to patient handling job while emergency medical services of the fire service personnel and private ambulance paramedics have been done (Conrad et al. 2008) in which design of new EMS patient handling devices offers potential intervention opportunity for combating the problem. With the help of an ecological model of musculoskeletal injuries in fire service, they have considered 25 paramedics/firefighter from 13 suburban departments. Considering different types of EMS patient handling scenario they have made three groups. Each group focused on two sessions: one session to brainstorm ideas for device and second session to validate sketches of their design ideas and they have analyzed these sketches with the help of industrial engineer. The results of the study were getting worthy design ideas for the EMS patient handling devices.

In the analysis of the effect of changing patient handling tasks, nine female healthcare workers are subjects who performed eight different tasks involving moving turning and lifting jobs (Schibye et al. 2003). The task has been done in two sessions: in first session healthcare workers have done the patient handling job using their own preferred techniques without any instruction whereas in second session they have only used the recommended techniques. A dynamic 3D biomechanical model has been used for calculation of torque and forces at L4/L5 joint by using force platform and video system. ANOVA is used in the analysis of the data in their study. The results of the study were found that the mechanical load was reduced below 3400 N for all the tasks using a recommended patient handling techniques.

8.2.1 Problems and Research Issues

The nursing staff involved in patient handling jobs may face many types of complex problems because of their awkward working postures during manual transfer of patients. Using inappropriate devices, equipment or methods for patient handling and lack of proper training for the equipment use may also be the reasons for such problems. The main problems as experienced by the nursing staff are as follows:

i. **Musculoskeletal disorders (MSDs)** such as back, knee, shoulder, or neck injury and carpal tunnel syndrome (Prairie et al. 2016; Prairie and Corbeil 2014; Ramos et al. 2014; Long et al. 2012; Kee and Seo 2007; Armstrong et al. 2017),
ii. **Anthropometric mismatch** between the nursing staff and equipment (Botha and Bridger 1998; Stanton et al. 2004; Warming et al. 2009; Lima et al. 2015),
iii. **Enormous Physical Stress** resulting in fatigue and damages in the human body, either temporary or permanent (Waters et al. 1993; Saha and Ray 2017; Mehta et al. 2011),
iv. **Poor Level of Human Performance** due to adverse environmental conditions and occupational hazards (Saha and Ray 2017; Santos et al. 2016), and
v. **Lack of Work Diversity** leading to ergonomic risk factors (Amell et al. 2002).

8.2.2 Existing Approaches for Evaluation

Some of the important modeling approaches which may be used in manual patient handling jobs are briefly explained below.

8.2.2.1 Biomechanical Evaluation

A biomechanical model is used to calculate and analyze the forces and torques on the segment of the body with the help of Ariel Performance Analysis System (APAS). The video taken by the digital camera of manual patient handling jobs is used in APAS to measure the forces and torques experienced by the different parts of the body and compare these forces and torques with the standard muscle strength limitation to find out the critical posture and part of the body where exerted forces and torques are exceeded the given limit (Ray et al. 2015; Schibye et al. 2003). Types of biomechanical model are as follows:

i. **Static Biomechanical Model**
   Analysis of the forces on the human body without consideration of the motion of the body, i.e., the calculation of force keeping the body in rest is called static biomechanical model (Owen et al. 1992; Ray et al. 2015).
ii. **Dynamic Biomechanical Model**
   Analysis of forces on the human body keeping the body in motion is called dynamic biomechanical model (Skotte et al. 2002; Schibye et al. 2003; Stanton et al. 2004; Lorente et al. 2016).

8.2.2.2 Physical Evaluation

In general, the musculoskeletal injuries begins with the workers discomfort. Sensations of discomfort of body are early warning of the musculoskeletal disease and it adversely affects the performance of the worker such a way that there are either decrease in quality of work through an increase in error rate or decrease in quantity of work or both will occur together. Physical method is used to assess the musculoskeletal discomfort through making a survey. These surveys are self-reported reported survey because discomfort cannot be directly observed or measured (Stanton et al. 2004; Hignett et al. 2016; Yuan et al. 2016; Nichols 1999; Oakman and Chan 2015).

These are some method used to assess the discomfort of the workers.

i. PLIBEL: This method consists of a critical checklist of items obtained through the comprehensive study of literature related to ergonomics. With the help of these checkpoints, workers can assess ergonomic hazards at the workplace and they can identify the musculoskeletal stress factors which may have injurious effects (Stanton et al. 2004).

ii. National Institute of Operational Safety and Health (NIOSH): A list of questionnaires made by NIOSH is used to assess the physical stresses and discomfort at the workplaces. This is also a self-reported measure of musculoskeletal discomfort. This method is generally used for the epidemiologic research or surveillance purposes (Bartnicka 2015).
iii. The Dutch Musculoskeletal Questionnaire (DMQ): DMQ is used to measure work-related musculoskeletal discomfort risk factor and symptoms. The standard version of questionnaire used in DMQ consists of 9 pages and 25 questions per page which are to be filled by worker themselves within the time interval of 30 min (Stanton et al. 2004).

8.2.2.3 Physiological Evaluation

Physiological method is used to measure human physiology. Mental workload can be determined by the interaction of operator and task. The operator may have some other activity while doing their duties, for example, using mobile during driving the car by the driver may increase the mental stress of the driver; the mental stress can be decreased by the decreasing the speed. Mental stress can be known by the measuring the heart rate with the help of Galvanic Skin Response (GSR) and blood pressure (Waters et al. 1993; Stanton et al. 2004; Barrett and Dennis 2005).

8.2.3 Critical Appraisal of the Existing Approaches

Patient handling jobs are the critical jobs in healthcare system where many times the nursing staff use to transfer the patient manually and experience problems like musculoskeletal diseases. Some of the researchers in Healthcare system have developed the model to minimize the musculoskeletal diseases and to give the comfort to the patient.

One of these models is two-dimensional biomechanical model: This model is based on the static equilibrium of the body. The summation of all the forces at a particular point in x- and y-directions respectively is zero. The summation of the moment at a particular point is also zero considering that point is not rotating with respect to any other point on the body.

Another model is a dynamic 3D biomechanical model to evaluate low back loading for the common patient handling tasks.

In three-dimensional biomechanical model, Three-Dimensional Static Strength Prediction Progam (3DSSPP) software is used which has the following properties:

i. It predicts the static strength requirements for the job such as lifting, pushing, pressing, and pulling;
ii. It is used to evaluate the shear and compressive forces at L5/S1 during manual material handling jobs;

iii. It can be used to evaluate the proposed workplace designs and redesigns prior to actual construction of the workplace;
iv. This model is applicable to three-dimensional motion of workers; and
v. In this model there is an assumption that the acceleration and momentum are negligible; therefore, it is the most useful model for slow movement of worker and heavy material lifting.

Biomechanical model also can be used as semi-dynamically in which the inertia effect is neglected for one or more segments of the body.

Emergency Medical Services (EMS) model is used to generate a beginning idea for the new EMS patient handling devices that were framed within contextual reality of the end user in EMS.

Intervention for patient handling equipment can be used by the nursing staff to improve the comfort of use of equipment and also to improve their general health and reduce musculoskeletal problems in patient handling jobs.

EMG-assisted model and biomechanical model are used to investigate the difference between peak external hand forces and external moments generated at L5/S1 joint at low back due to maneuvering-loaded floor-based and overhead-mounted patient devices.

8.3 A Comprehensive Framework for Biomechanical Evaluation of Patient Handling Jobs

The systematic review of the literature has been done and identified the problem in the healthcare being faced by the nursing personnel such as back, knee, shoulder or neck injury, carpal tunnel syndrome, enormous physical stress, anthropometric mismatch, and other problems. There are available models for the manual material handling jobs such as biomechanical model, physical model, and psychological model in ergonomics handbook (Stanton et al. 2004).

Patient handling activities like moving the patient from bed to stretcher, stretcher to bed, stretcher to ambulance, ambulance to stretcher, toilet to wheelchair, wheelchair to toilet, turning the patient on bed, moving the stretcher with patient from one place to another, etc. are very common in healthcare systems. These patient handling jobs may consist of poor and awkward work postures by the nursing staff, because of which the nursing staff may suffer from the fatigue and high level of physical stress. The nursing staff may have the problem like lower back pain and upper extremity pain. Considering these types of problems in healthcare system while performing patient handling job, the development of framework should be such a way that the problems in the patient handling jobs can be easily identified and can minimize the problems of nursing staff as well as maximize the comfort of patient. To calculate the criticality of body postures

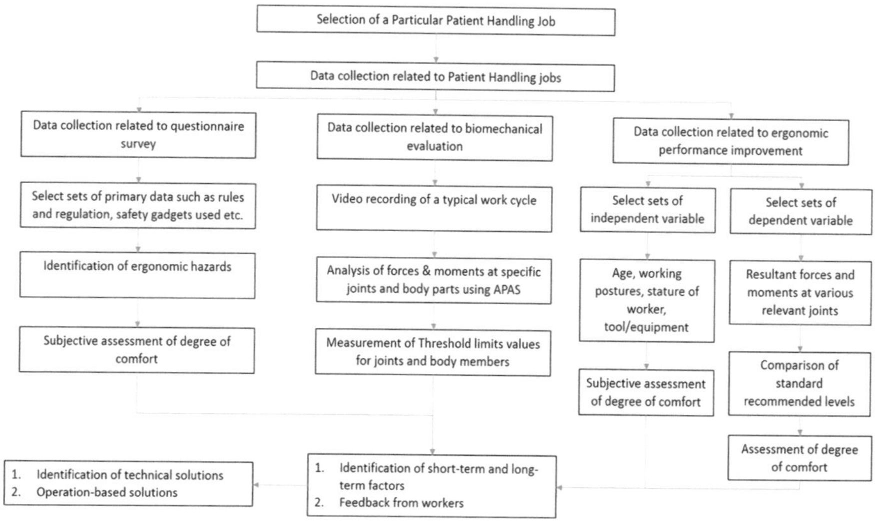

Fig. 8.11 A comprehensive framework for biomechanical evaluation of patient handling jobs

biomechanical model is very helpful; it may identify the critical body joints where the improvement is needed. With the help of this biomechanical model the evaluation of critical body joints in critical body postures of the nursing staff will be done.

A comprehensive framework for biomechanical evaluation as proposed is explained in Fig. 8.11.

The framework consists of a number of interrelated steps. The steps are briefly explained below.

Step-I: Selection of various Patient Handling Jobs

There are various types of patient handling jobs as mentioned in the introduction part. One of the patient handling jobs will be selected and data will be collected related to questionnaire survey, biomechanical evaluation, and ergonomic performance improvement.

Step-II: Data Collection

(i) Data Collection Related to Questionnaire Survey

A set of questionnaire will be made relevant to the selected patient handling jobs and activities carried out in that patient handling job. The questionnaire survey will be carried out through the systematic collection of data. The collection of data will be taken in the following two phases:

a. Preliminary data collection:

This data collection is necessary for an understanding of the work system. It consists of

i. Types of activities against each type of patient handling jobs,
ii. Types of tools, mechanical aids, and other handling tools used in patient handling jobs,
iii. Types of safety gadgets being used/recommended for nursing staff,
iv. Types of problems being faced or reported by the concerned nursing staff,
v. Work postures and body movement for the different activities carried out by the concerned nursing staff, and
vi. Rules and regulation/Standards which are used for the patient handling jobs.

These types of data will be collected with the help of discussion with the concerned person, past records of data and direct observation.

b. Evaluation-related detailed data collection:

This is the questionnaire-based survey in which two sets of questionnaires will be made, one related to the personal details of the concerned nursing person who are engaged in the patient handling jobs which consist of questions such as work conditions, kinds of jobs, and contractual obligations. In the second set of questionnaire related to the ergonomic problem experienced by the nursing personal, it consists of questions like characteristics of patient handling jobs, types of tools and techniques, types of occupational health problem, etc.

(ii) **Data Collection—Related to Biomechanical Evaluation**

The video of the different patient handling jobs will be taken by the high-quality camera for different nursing personals for a specific work cycle. The anthropometric data such that height, age, weight of the object carried out by nursing personal, and other relevant data for the every concerned nursing personal will be collected before every work cycle. These data will be used in Ariel Performance Analysis System (APAS) and analyze the forces and moments at specific joints and body parts.

Step-III: Analysis of Data

The data collected through questionnaire survey will be used to find out the problem bearing with the nursing staff while carrying patient handling jobs. PLIBEL, NIOSH, and DMQ questionnaire survey will be conducted and will identify the most critical problems which are facing by the nursing staff. The biomechanical analysis will be done in this with the help of Ariel Performance Analysis System (APAS).

The steps which are used in the APAS will be as follows:

i. Video recording of the nursing personal using high-quality camera while performing the specific patient handling jobs, e.g., moving the patient from bed to wheel chair;
ii. Selection of the length of the video which is to be analyzed;
iii. Selection of the digitalized video in the APAS software;
iv. Selection of reference coordinates;
v. Selection of control points and body parts need to be analyzed;
vi. Join the control points using straight line to develop working postures for each frame and verify the selection for the selected work cycle;
vii. Select the appropriate tab for force and angular momentum analysis;
viii. Store the result and plot the graph between desired parameters using 'using plot option';
ix. Analyze the data using the data, graph and movement of the worker simultaneously using 'multiple windows' option; and
x. Derive appropriate conclusion based on the result obtained.

Step-IV: Selection of Alternative Design of Workstation

After the analysis of data and problem identified in the existing work system, the changes in the work system will be done through the intervention of new patient handling devices to minimize the manual handling of the patient. The nursing staff will be trained for proper working postures while patient handling jobs will also educate to handle the new patient handling devices.

Step-V: Action Steps for Implementation

Following are the action steps for implementation:

i. Finding problems by using questionnaire survey and biomechanical analysis;
ii. Making the design changes in the work system;
iii. Intervention of different types of patient handling devices;
iv. Arrangement of training program of nursing staff related to patient handling devices and existing worksystem.

8.4 Conclusions

The systematic review of the literature on patient handling jobs in healthcare systems has been done in this paper. The nursing staff of healthcare systems are facing problems like musculoskeletal disorders, back injury, knee injury, shoulder injury, neck injury, carpal tunnel syndrome, enormous physical stress, anthropometric mismatch, etc. has been identified as per the existing healthcare ergonomic literature. The ergonomic hazards which are faced by the nursing staff can be identified by the methods available in the literature such as PLIBEL, NIOSH, and DMQ questionnaire surveys. To minimize these problems of the nursing staff different types of models have been identified in the literature such as biomechanical model, physical model, and psychological model.

References

Amell, T. K., Kumar, S., & Rosser, B. W. J. (2002). Ergonomics, loss management, and occupational injury and illness surveillance. Part 2: injury and illness incident profile. sample data. *International Journal of Industrial Ergonomics, 29*(4), 199–210.

Armstrong, D. P., et al. (2017). Implementing powered stretcher and load systems was a cost effective intervention to reduce the incidence rates of stretcher related injuries in a paramedic service. *Applied Ergonomics, 62,* 34–42.

Barrett, R. S., & Dennis, G. J. (2005). Ergonomic issues in team lifting. *Human Factors and Ergonomics In Manufacturing, 15*(3), 293–307.

Bartnicka, J. (2015) Knowledge-based ergonomic assessment of working conditions in surgical ward—a case study. Safety Science 71(PB): 178–188.

Botha, W. E., & Bridger, R. S. (1998). Anthropometric variability, equipment usability and musculoskeletal pain in a group of nurses in the Western Cape. *Applied Ergonomics, 29*(6), 481–490.

Conrad, K. M., et al. (2008). Designing ergonomic interventions for EMS workers: concept generation of patient-handling devices. *Applied Ergonomics, 39*(6), 792–802.

Cooper, G., & Ghassemieh, E. (2007). Risk assessment of patient handling with ambulance stretcher systems (ramp/(winch), easi-loader, tail-lift) using biomechanical failure criteria. *Medical Engineering and Physics, 29*(7), 775–787.

Dutta, T., et al. (2012). A biomechanical assessment of floor and overhead lifts using one or two caregivers for patient transfers. *Applied Ergonomics, 43*(3), 521–531.

Elford, W., Straker, L., & Strauss, G. (2000). Patient handling with and without slings: an analysis of the risk of injury to the lumbar spine. *Applied Ergonomics, 31*(2), 185–200.

Garg, A., & Owen, B. (1994). Prevention of back injuries in healthcare workers. *International Journal of Industrial Ergonomics, 14*(4), 315–331.

Hignett, S., Edmunds Otter, M., & Keen, C. (2016). Safety risks associated with physical interactions between patients and caregivers during treatment and care delivery in home care settings: a systematic review. *International Journal of Nursing Studies, 59,* 1–14.

Hignett, S. & Richardson, B. (1997). Manual handling human loads in a hospital: An exploratory study to identify nurses' perceptions . Applied Ergonomics, 26(3), 221–226: Hignett, S. & Richardson B. (1995). *Journal of Safety Research*, *28*(2), 116–117.

Holstrom, E., Lindell, J. & MO&Z, U. (1993). Healthy lower backs in the construction industry in Sweden, Work & Stress *7*, 259–271.

Kee, D., & Seo, S. R. (2007). Musculoskeletal disorders among nursing personnel in Korea. *International Journal of Industrial Ergonomics, 37*(3), 207–212.

Le Bon, C., & Forrester, C. (1997). An ergonomic evaluation of a patient handling device: the elevate and transfer vehicle. *Applied Ergonomics, 28*(5–6), 365–374.

Lima, R. et al. (2015). Ergonomics, anthropometrics, and kinetic evaluation of gait: A case study. *Procedia Manufacturing*, 3(Ahfe), 4370–4376. Available Lindbeck, L. & Engkvist, I.-L. (1993). Biomechanical analysis of 2 patient handling tasks. *International Journal of Industrial Ergonomics*, *12*(1–2), 117–125.

Long, M. H., Johnston, V., & Bogossian, F. (2012). Work-related upper quadrant musculoskeletal disorders in midwives, nurses and physicians: A systematic review of risk factors and functional consequences. *Applied Ergonomics, 43*(3), 455–467.

Lorente, D. et al. (2016). A framework for modelling the biomechanical behaviour of the human liver during breathing in real time using machine learning. *Expert Systems with Applications* (Vol. 71, pp. 342–357). Available at: http://linkinghub.elsevier.com/retrieve/pii/S0957417416306728.

Mehta, R. K., et al. (2011). Ergonomic evaluation of hospital bed design features during patient handling tasks. *International Journal of Industrial Ergonomics, 41*(6), 647–652.

Nichols, S. (1999). Physical ergonomics issues of virtual environment use. *Applied Ergonomics, 30,* 79–90.

Oakman, J., & Chan, S. (2015). Risk management: Where should we target strategies to reduce work-related musculoskeletal disorders? *Safety Science, 73,* 99–105.

Owen, B. D., Garg, A., & Jensen, R. C. (1992). Four methods for identification of most back-stressing tasks performed by nursing assistants in nursing homes. *International Journal of Industrial Ergonomics, 9*(3), 213–220.

Owen, B. (1988). Patient handling devices: an ergonomic approach to lifting patients. *In Trends in Ergonomics/Human Factors* V, ed. F. Aghazadeh, pp. 721–729. Elsevier Science.

Prairie, J., et al. (2016). Biomechanical risk assessment during field loading of hydraulic stretchers into ambulances. *International Journal of Industrial Ergonomics, 54,* 1–9.

Prairie, J., & Corbeil, P. (2014). Paramedics on the job: Dynamic trunk motion assessment at the workplace. *Applied Ergonomics, 45*(4), 895–903.

Ramos, D. G., Arezes, P. M. & Afonso, P. (2014). Analysis of the return on preventive measures in musculoskeletal disorders through the benefit-cost ratio: A case study in a hospital. *International Journal of Industrial Ergonomics*.

Ray, P. K., Parida, R. & Sarkar, S. (2015). Ergonomic Analysis of construction jobs in India: A biomechanical modelling approach. *Procedia Manufacturing*, 3(Ahfe), 4606–4612.

Risr, B. W., et al. (2017). A multi-component patient-handling intervention improves attitudes and behaviors for safe patient handling and reduces aggression experienced by nursing staff: A controlled before-after study. *Applied Ergonomics, 60,* 74–82.

Roffey, D. M. et al. (2010). Causal assessment of workplace manual handling or assisting patients and low back pain: Results of a systematic review. *The spine journal : official journal of the North American Spine Society*, *10*(7), 639–651. Available at: http://dx.doi.org/10.1016/j.spinee.2010.04.028

Saha, E. & Ray, P. (2017). Ergonomic performance measurement system of work-systems in healthcare. In *Advances in Human Factors and Ergonomics*. pp. 67–74.

Santos, A. L. R., et al. (2016). Safety challenges of medical equipment in nurse anaesthetist training in Haiti. *Applied Ergonomics, 53,* 110–121.

Schibye, B., et al. (2003). Biomechanical analysis of the effect of changing patient-handling technique. *Applied Ergonomics, 34*(2), 115–123.

Skotte, J. H., et al. (2002). A dynamic 3D biomechanical evaluation of the load on the low back during different patient-handling tasks. *Journal of Biomechanics, 35*(10), 1357–1366.

Stanton, N. et al. (2004). *Handbook of human factors and ergonomics methods*, Available at: http://video.yahoo.com/watch/111582/992708.

Szeto, G. P. Y., et al. (2013). A study of spinal kinematics in community nurses performing nursing tasks. *International Journal of Industrial Ergonomics, 43*(3), 203–209.

Waaijer, E. M. (2014, July). Ergonomics, manual handling of people in the healthcare sector international consensus (Cen/ ISO Technical Report (TR) 12296—2013). *International Journal of Industrial Ergonomics*, 44, pp. 3296–3299.

Warming, S., et al. (2009). Musculoskeletal complaints among nurses related to patient handling tasks and psychosocial factors—Based on logbook registrations. *Applied Ergonomics, 40*(4), 569–576.

Waters, T. R., et al. (1993). Revised NIOSH equation for the design and evaluation of manual lifting tasks. *Ergonomics, 36*(7), 749–776.

Yuan, L., et al. (2016). An integrated biomechanical modeling approach to the ergonomic evaluation of drywall installation. *Applied Ergonomics, 53,* 52–63.

Chapter 9
Modeling and Analysis of Distribution of Blood Stocks to Healthcare Units

Pratiksha Patil, Pradip Kumar Ray and Esha Saha

Abstract The problem of both under stock and over stock of blood due to seasonal variations in blood requirements is a serious problem affecting any blood distribution system in India and other countries. There may be lack of coordination between blood banks and its supply system. In this context, supply chain management may assume a significant role and has attracted serious research attention over the past few years. A literature review reveals a considerable spurt in research in theory and practice of SCM. An integrated supply chain and distribution system as an extended enterprise is to be developed for addressing the problems related to mismatch between supply and demand of blood stocks at a particular period of time with respect to a given population of patients in a location. This paper presents a model wherein the blood stocks are redistributed from one blood bank to another with the assurance of meeting the minimum level demand at emergency situation avoiding stockout situation. Demand has been estimated and forecasted considering the seasonality and trend factor in account. In this model, the blood banks considered are clustered using k-means clustering technique based on the distances between the blood banks. The blood banks with excess of stock, considered as centroid, are to distribute the excess stock to the blood banks with scarcity. The main objective of the paper is to determine the stocking rules of blood so as to reduce the wastage of the blood units and reducing the scarcity at demand points.

Keywords Blood supply chain management · Clustering algorithm · Forecasting

---

P. Patil · P.K. Ray (✉) · E. Saha
Department of Industrial and Systems Engineering,
Indian Institute of Technology Kharagpur, Kharagpur 721302, India
e-mail: pkr@vgsom.iitkgp.ernet.in

P.K. Ray and J. Maiti (eds.), *Healthcare Systems Management: Methodologies and Applications*, Managing the Asian Century,
DOI 10.1007/978-981-10-5631-4_9

9.1 Introduction

Blood transfusion therapy is an important aspect of the medical care system, and it has been stated that one in three infants, teens, and adults of all ages will need blood transfusion at one point of their life. To meet the blood demand, blood collection centers and hospital blood banks must maintain desirable inventory levels to ensure that blood demand is adequately met and appropriate measures are taken to minimize blood waste. There is a need of effective and efficient management of the blood supply, as human blood is a perishable product. To ensure effective use of the limited blood resources, blood utilization and inventory management policies must be practiced by the blood collection centers, hospital blood banks, and physicians ordering transfusions. Blood is an inherent requirement for health care and proper functioning of the health system. NACO is primarily responsible for ensuring provision of safe blood for India since 1992. A network of 1131 blood banks across the country in over 600 districts are being supported by NACO and aspired to achieve accessibility to adequate quantity of safe, quality and affordable blood and blood components to the needy. Government of India adopted the National Blood Policy in April 2002 which aims to develop a nationwide system to ensure easy access to adequate and safe and good quality blood supply. Supreme Court judgment of 1996 for CWP 91/1992 commissioned creating of National Blood Transfusion Council and elimination of professional blood donation. National Blood Transfusion Council (NBTC), the apex policy making body for issues pertaining to blood and plasma is a part of National AIDS Control Organization.

Accordingly, all through the phases of the National AIDS Control Programme, an inclusive, efficient, and total quality management approach has been adopted toward strengthening Blood Banks and Blood Transfusion Services. NACO has taken number of steps towards the modernization of blood banks in the country by providing the critical inputs for ensuring provision of safe blood for the country. During this time HIV sero-reactivity among blood donors also declined to 0.14% in NACO-supported Blood Banks. Availability of Blood has increased to 10.8 million blood units in 2015–2016.

It is important that every pint of blood donated should end up as a transfusable product. The blood supply chain is made up mainly of blood donors, regional blood centers, (community blood banks, or hospital blood bank donor rooms), hospital blood banks, and patients at the hospital. In the blood center or hospital blood bank donor room blood is collected in units of one pint from donors at a collection site. The collected blood undergoes a multiple series of typing and screening tests, is stored at the Blood Center or Blood Bank, and then shipped to a hospital blood bank or transfusion facility at the latter's request to satisfy present or expected demand for transfusions. Collection of blood is a crucial function in the supply chain. Blood donations are collected by scheduled visits to organizations, schools, or churches where donors have already pledged to give blood or telemarketers book platelet donors at scheduled times, walk-in donors to blood center's facilities and invited donors from a campaign.

9.1.1 The Blood Donation Process

Donating blood is a safe process. A sterile needle is used only once for each donor and then discarded. The blood donation process is described in the following points.

i. Blood donation is a simple four-step process: registration, medical history and mini-physical, donation and refreshments.
ii. A mini-physical is given to every blood donor, checking the donor's temperature, blood pressure, pulse and hemoglobin to ensure it is safe for the donor to give blood.
iii. The actual blood donation typically takes less than 10–12 min. The entire process, from the time you arrive to the time you leave, takes about an hour and 15 min.
iv. The average adult has about 10 units of blood in his body. Roughly 1 unit is given during a donation.
v. A healthy donor may donate red blood cells every 56 days, or double red cells every 112 days.
vi. A healthy donor can donate a maximum of 24 times a year. Also the donation of the platelets can be done as few as 7 days apart,
vii. Before transfusing the blood to patients, all donated blood is tested for HIV, hepatitis B and C, syphilis, and other infectious diseases.

However, there are various health reasons that an uncertain percentage of donors that pledge to donate blood may not be able to donate. Hence the amount to be collected may only be estimated. Whole blood, packed red blood cells, packed red blood cells leukocytes reduced, fresh frozen plasma, plasma cryoprecipitate, and platelets (apheresis and random),these are the primary blood products. We can extract packed red blood cells (RBCs), plasma, and random platelets (RDP), from a whole blood unit drawn from a donor and prepared by centrifugal or gravitational separation as shown in Fig. 9.1.

Platelets are required and needed to support cancer therapy, treatment of blood disorders, organ transplants, and open-heart surgery. Unpredictable effects may occur from the deficiencies in platelet number and function in a patient that may range from major life-threatening hemorrhage to clinically insignificant prolongation of the bleeding time. Blood is a product of unique medical value. It is

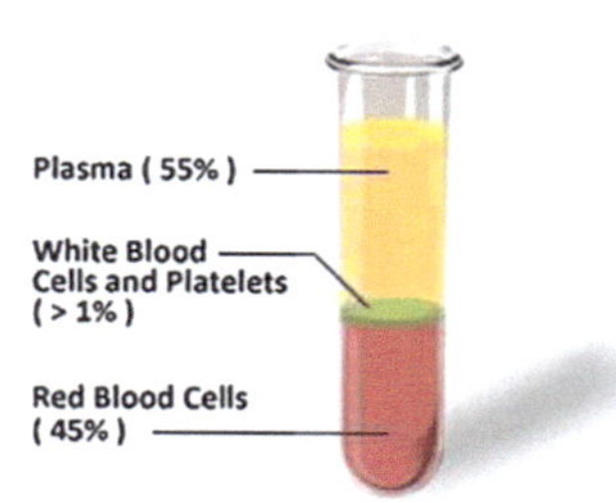

Fig. 9.1 Blood Components extracted from Whole Blood unit

perishable and its usable lifetime value is of 21 days. Supply and demand are stochastic in nature.

9.1.2 Importance of Supply Chain for Blood Bank

As a supply chain, the flow of blood and blood products from the donor to the patient would seem to be one of the simplest inventory and distribution problems in the supply chain literature. The whole blood from donors is collected, processed it into its components at a regional blood center or a community blood center and delivered the components to hospitals where they are transfused into patients. The problem is interesting and difficult from a research perspective because of the following reasons. First, blood is a perishable commodity and whole blood has many components, each of which has a different shelf life before it perishes. The preparation of different components involves significant costs. Second, the supply of whole blood at a donor drawing location is a random variable that often has a large variance, and for planning purposes, the donor drawing locations and drawing dates are themselves sometimes random variables. The supply is also impacted by the need to screen out a growing list of viruses and diseases before the blood and its components may be used for transfusions; more variability and more risks are introduced. Third, the demands for blood components at a hospital in both their amounts and frequency are random variables. Fourth, many interacting decisions must be made at the strategic design, strategic policies, and operational and tactical levels. All are affected by the need to control costs, to minimize outdating and waste and, above all, to control potential shortages. Fifth, the entire blood supply chain can be examined as an essentially whole system and not just a subsystem of some larger system as occurs in most other supply chains. And finally, from a research perspective, generalizable theoretical research may be extracted from the real problem regarding perishable inventories and regarding disease testing.

9.1.3 The Need of a Blood Bank

A blood bank is a center where blood gathered as a result of blood donation, stored and preserved for later use in blood transfusion. The term ‘blood bank’ typically refers to a division of a hospital, where the storage of blood product occurs and where proper testing is performed to reduce the risk of transfusion related adverse events. However, it may also be referred to as a collection center. Blood banks constitute a vital part of health services. Their logistics include blood procurement, processing, cross matching, storage, distribution, recycling, pricing, quality control, and outdating. Blood Bank should maintain adequate inventory levels to meet patient demand, keep blood wastage to a minimum, provide blood of high quality and keep original operating costs at an acceptable level. A supply chain is a network of supplier, manufacturing, assembly, distribution, and logistics facilities that perform the functions of procurement of materials, transformation of these materials into intermediate and finished products and the distribution of these products to customers.

9.1.4 Few Facts of Blood Needs in India

Few facts about the blood needs in India are discussed in the following points:

i. Every year our nation requires about 5 crore units of blood, out of which only a meager 2.5 crore units of blood are available.
ii. There is no substitute for human blood.
iii. Every two seconds someone needs blood.
iv. More than 38,000 blood donations are needed every day.
v. A total of 30 million blood components are transfused each year.
vi. The average red blood cell transfusion is approximately 3 pints.
vii. The blood type most often requested by hospitals is Type O.
viii. More than 1 million new people are diagnosed with cancer each year. Many of those cancer patients will need blood, sometimes daily, during their chemotherapy treatment.
ix. A single car accident victim can require as many as 100 units of blood.
x. Type O-negative blood (red cells) can be transfused to patients of all blood types. The blood group type O− is always in great demand and often in short supply.
xi. Type AB-positive plasma can be transfused to patients of all other blood types. AB plasma is also usually in short supply.

9.1.5 Problems in Storing Blood Stock at the Blood Bank

Balancing blood stocks is a very complex issue that requires constant monitoring and actions on the part of the blood transfusion service. The availability of the blood stocks not only depends on blood donors and the blood collected, but also depends on the consumption of blood. The volumes of blood components required as well as blood groups are unpredictable. In cases of increased needs for blood, additional blood drives are also being organized along with those of regular ones. Donors are targeted over the telephone, generally, when certain blood groups are missing, and as an extreme measure, the blood transfusion service makes a public call to blood donors in the media. However, the lack of blood is not only the problem in blood transfusion. There also exists the problem of stockpiling. Since blood components have a certain shelf life, i.e., they have an expiry date. In such cases, only a limited number of donors are accepted at a blood drive or the latter is postponed. The stock of blood is maintained in a healthy condition to meet the demand. As the commodity is perishable in nature, the policies that matter regarding inventory management are maintaining average inventory level, average age of blood during transfusion, and average amount of blood that perishes.

The objective of the paper is to (i) increase the availability of the blood in any given blood bank by reallocating and redistributing of the blood stocks, (ii) decrease the lead time to reach the demand point from the supply point, and (iii) reduce the blood stock wastage. The parameters considered are the demand at every blood bank which is estimated using a time series model, the minimum stock and maximum stock amount, number of clusters to be formed, and the lead time of transferring blood units from one blood bank to another.

9.2 Review of Literature

The review of existing literature regarding supply chain of blood bank is classified on various aspects, such as blood bank supply chain and its importance, forecasting demand and supply, and blood inventory management and is discussed in the following subsections.

9.2.1 Comprehensive Review on Blood Bank Supply Chain

Supply chain management (SCM) is the management of the flow of goods. It includes the movement and storage of raw materials, work-in-process inventory, and finished goods from point of origin to point of consumption. The end customers of supply chain require the network to be interconnected or interlinked, channels and node businesses to be involved in the provision of products and services. Supply chain management has been defined as the design, planning, execution, control, and monitoring of supply chain activities with the objective of creating net value, building a competitive infrastructure, influencing the worldwide logistics, synchronizing supply with demand and measuring performance globally. SCM draws heavily from the areas of operations management, logistics, procurement, and information technology, and strives for an integrated approach.

Several authors have considered problems, such as facility location, set covering, allocation, capacity planning, routing, and supply chain management to address the design and optimization of supply chains of blood or other perishable critical products (Brandeau et al. 2004; Atkinson et al. 2012). In addition, inventory management problems in blood supply chain is considered by Dillon et al. (2017), Hosseinifard and Abbasi (2016), Puranam et al. (2017) and Haijema (2014). The problems related to supply chain design for effective and efficient blood supply is considered by Fahimnia et al. (2017), Yang and Liu (2017), Jabbarzadeh et al.

(2014), Pierskalla (2004). The problem on integrated procurement, production, and distribution in platelet supply chain is considered by Ensafian and Yaghoubi (2017).

9.2.2 Forecasting Demand and Supply

A reliable and trustable forecast of the quantity and timing of future blood supply (collection from donors) and blood demand from hospital blood banks is needed for the management of inventory at the Regional Blood Center and making an effective decision on blood inventory control. Forecasting blood supply and demand can be based on quantitative approaches (using historical data to predict the future using regression or time series analysis) and qualitative approaches (using expert judgment or management assumptions).

The forecasting model is made of blood transfusion forecasts using an exponential smoothing model (this method exponentially decreases weights of past data); blood expiration forecasts using an exponential function with empirically derived parameters; blood collection forecasts using historical data; and blood inventory projection based on the transfusion forecast, predicted expirations, and forecasted collections.

The Box–Jenkins forecasting models uses a variable's past behavior to select the best forecasting model from a general class of models including autoregressive, moving average, autoregressive-moving average (ARIMA), and multiple regression models for forecasting the aggregate number of blood tests to be conducted. The regression models gives significantly better forecast errors for both short- and long-range horizons. Pereira (2004) used three time series (namely autoregressive integrated moving average (ARIMA), the Holt-Winters family of exponential smoothing models, and one neural network-based) methods to investigate the forecasting of demand for red blood cell transfusion.

Even though forecasting is a precondition for decision-making in inventory practice, few studies have focused on the interactions between forecasting and inventory decisions. Croston (1972) have concluded that forecast errors can distort projections of customer service. In a study conducted on the impact of forecasting on inventory decisions in a large physical distribution system, it is concluded that the forecasting model choice is an important factor in determining the amount of investment to support any target level of customer service. Analyzing the characteristics of the inventory demand time series to identify alternative forecasting models, and the experimental design to test forecasting models are relevant in modeling and analysis of distribution of blood stocks to healthcare units.

The errors of time series forecast can be calculated using: Mean-Squared Error (MSE) which is the absolute error that squares the difference between the actual historical data and the forecast-fitted data predicted by the model, Root Mean-Squared Error (RMSE) which is the average of the absolute values of the forecast errors, Mean Absolute Deviation (MAD) which is an error statistic that averages the absolute value of the difference between the actual historical data and the forecast-fitted data predicted by the model and Mean Absolute Percent Error (MAPS) which is a relative error statistic measured as an average percent error of the historical data points.

9.2.3 Blood Inventory Management

The optimal allocation of blood inventory could be described as a problem of finding an issuing policy which either maximizes or minimizes a function of the inventory level and actions over time. Optimal selection of an issuing policy with conditions under which either FIFO (first in, first out) or LIFO (last in, first out) are used have generated a lot of interest especially with perishable products like blood. Hospitals ordering blood products from blood banks or blood centers insist on receiving the most fresh blood product, thereby forcing the blood bank or center to practice LIFO. Though the blood bank or center will prefer to send out the older units first (FIFO) to minimize outdate and shortage of blood products.

An optimal sequence to remove items from a stockpile of finite units of varying ages has been formulated. The stockpile which is consisting of n items is being associated with the ith item having an age (length of time in the stockpile) Si (1, *n*). The total field life (a function L(S) of the age) of the stockpile depends on the sequence in which items are removed from the stockpile, as an item was issued only when the previous item issued had expired. They stated that if a complete knowledge of the function L(S) was available, then optimal policies for any given situation could be obtained by a consideration of all n factorial different orderings and the consequent selection of the best, or the use of an algorithm would lead to the solution. First in, first out (FIFO) and last in, first out (LIFO) issuing policies in practice are the most easily understood and the most easily implemented inventory policies, and only knowledge of the relative ages of the items in the inventory are required. In perishable product inventory systems where the issuing of the stock to meet demand was controlled by the consumer, the movement of units through the system, obeying of LIFO issuing policy has been found. Fries (1975) determined independently the optimal ordering policy for a product with a general lifetime of m periods by solving a dynamic programming equation. Numerous theoretical models have been developed using dynamic programming models, queuing models and Markov chain models to solve the blood inventory problem. Simulation models have been used also to determine the operating characteristics curves and decision rules for setting optimal blood inventory levels. Belien and Force (2012), Prastacos (1984) carried out a comprehensive review of the theory and practice of blood inventory management and the models developed to address some of the issues faced at the hospital levels. Due to the assumption that all units demanded are used in these analytical research on general perishable products, the analytical results obtained are not directly applicable to blood inventory management (Prastacos 1984). Due to this drawback blood bankers turned to empirically obtained results in combination with their own experience.

Some of the recent studies on perishables include the use of an estimator for the probability that an item will be sold in a period to determine the outdated and shortage operating curves in an inventory problem with a fixed lifetime (Omosigho 2002).

After referring various research works in the field of Supply Chain of Blood Bank, it can be concluded that Blood service operations are a key component of the healthcare system all over the world. Still the research in this field is lacking due to their associated unique challenges. Its usable lifetime value is of 21 days and Supply and Demand of blood are stochastic in nature. The supply chain of a blood bank is different from conventional supply chains in the form that the product is perishable. Not only is its procurement and delivery important but also its disposal in case it is rendered non-meritorious.

9.3 Forecasting Blood Collection and Demand

Time Series Analysis are statistical techniques used when several years' data for a product or product line are available and when relationships and trends are both clear and relatively stable. One of the basic principles of statistical forecasting—indeed, of all forecasting when historical data are available—is that the forecaster should use the data on past performance to get a projection of the current rate (of sales, say) and of how fast this rate is increasing or decreasing. The current rate and changes in the rate—"acceleration" and "deceleration"—constitute the basis of forecasting. Various mathematical techniques can develop projections from them once they are known. The matter is not so simple as it sounds, however. To make projections from raw data since the rates and trends are not immediately obvious; they are mixed up with seasonal variations, for example, and perhaps distorted by such factors as the effects of a large sales promotion campaign. The raw data must be cleaned/smoothened before they are usable, and this is frequently done by time series analysis. Now, a time series is a set of chronologically ordered points of raw data—for example, a division's sales of a given product, by month, for several years. Time series analysis helps to identify and explain:

i. Any regularity or systematic variation in the series of data which is due to seasonality—the "seasonals".
ii. Cyclical patterns that repeat any two or three years or more.
iii. Trends in the data.
iv. Growth rates of these trends.

Most existing methods identify only the seasonals, the combined effect of trends and cycles, and the irregular, or chance, component. They do not separate trends from cycles. The RBC transfusion series was best fitted by a seasonal ARIMA (0, 1, 1) (0, 1, 1) (1, 2) model. Over 1-year time horizons, forecasts generated by ARIMA or exponential smoothing laid within the $\pm 10\%$ interval of the real RBC demand in 79% of months (62% in the case of neural networks). The coverage rate for the three methods was 89, 91, and 86%, respectively. Over 2-year time horizons, exponential smoothing largely outperformed the other methods. Predictions by exponential smoothing laid within the ±10% interval of real values in 75% of the 24 forecasted months, and the coverage rate was 87%. Over 1-year time horizons, predictions of RBC demand generated by ARIMA or exponential smoothing are accurate enough to be of help in the planning of blood collection efforts. For longer time horizons, exponential smoothing outperforms the other forecasting methods.

9.4 Blood Bank Inventory Management

The blood must be processed to be obtained some products, called blood components and blood products. Normally, the production is focused to produce the blood components. It is possible obtain four different types: Packed red blood cells (CH), Platelets (CP), Fresh frozen plasma (FFP), Cryoprecipitate (CRYO), Concentrate granulocytes (GC). These components have many uses, like the treatment of symptomatic anemia, coagulation disorders, thrombocytopenia, fibrinogen deficiency, and severe neutropenia, among other diseases. According to the Guide of Health Ministry of Brazil, 2011, one methodology to dimension the blood inventory is collecting the demand of the past 6 months and that number is divided by 180 and multiplied by three.

$$\mathrm{EM} = (\mathrm{NB}/180) * 3 \tag{9.1}$$

EM = Minimal stock;
NB = Number of blood bags demanded in the past 6 months.

However, this method is used at unusual situations, in normal conditions it is not applicable, because is necessary analyzes more detailed to the inferences can be aggregated to a forecast and inventory model more closely to the reality.

9.4.1 Models Applied in Blood Bank Inventory Management

In inventory management, some information is required, like the demand expected, numbers of orders, and the availability of the item. The inventory has some functions: economies of scale made possible due to the discount generated by the acquisition of large quantities or in gains related to production processes and transport; protection in order to protect the supply chain in cases of absence of items and advance is to meet anticipated demand. In the Blood Bank case, the use of the inventory is meet the demand, because this kind of product is irreplaceable and is used in emergency cases. The Blood Bank mission is guarantee that the blood components and the blood products being available to hospitals and emergency centers. To dimension an inventory management, some steps are suggested: (i) ABC inventory classification; (ii) defining the system parameters; and (iii) defining the safety stocks. According to these steps, the Pareto diagram can be used to understand the blood product importance. A model to define the stock level for most important blood products may be proposed using variables, such as safety stock and lead time of the process.

The model is formed by four equations to define the safety stock, the lead time process, the minimal stock, and the maximum stock. To define the safety stock, it is necessary to consider a service level required (NS). In this case, 99.99% of service level is considered for all blood products, due to the importance of having this product for many health treatments, where there is serious risk of life. The Eq. 9.2 shows how the safety stock is calculated.

$$\mathrm{SS} = \mathrm{SL} \times \mathrm{LT} \times \mathrm{SD} \tag{9.2}$$

where, SS = Safety stock; SL = service level required; LT = lead time of the process; SD = standard deviation. The lead time is obtained based on the timing of all process, showed in Eq. 9.3.

$$\mathrm{NLT} = \mathrm{Max\ LT} \times \mathrm{Max\ Demand} \tag{9.3}$$

where NLT = lead time necessary; Max LT = maximum process lead time; Max Demand = maximum demand value found in the time series data. Based on these equations, it is possible calculate the minimum and the maximum stock levels (Eqs. 9.4 and 9.5).

$$\mathrm{Minimum\ stock/Month} = \mathrm{SS} + \mathrm{NLT} \tag{9.4}$$

where Minimum/Month = minimum inventory level to be maintained for months; SS = safety stock; NLT = lead time necessary.

$$\mathrm{Maximum\ stock/Month} = \mathrm{Average} + \mathrm{Minimum\ stock/Month} \tag{9.5}$$

where Minimum stock/Month = minimum inventory level to be maintained for months; SS = safety stock;

It is important to say that this kind of inventory is composed by two sub models, called inventory assigned, when blood donations are directed to a specific receptor and unallocated inventory, that inventory in emergency appeal for unknown recipients. In emergency cases, the product must be released, even being assigned inventory, with the prospect of replacement. The same authors understand that it is necessary the maintenance the database of donors to call these donors to make new collection when necessary. Recent studies show that transfusing older blood may lead to increased mortality. This raises the issue of whether transfusing fresher blood can be achieved without jeopardizing blood availability.

A policy has been proposed that rather than transfusing the oldest available blood that is younger than 42 days, we transfuse the oldest blood that is younger than the threshold, and if there is no blood younger than the threshold then we transfuse the youngest blood that is older than the threshold. The proposed allocation policy with a threshold of 14 days could allow many Indian hospitals to significantly reduce the age of transfused blood, thereby possibly reducing morbidity and mortality, while having a negligible impact on supply chain operations.

9.4.2 Clustering: The Algorithm

K-means is one of the simplest unsupervised learning algorithms that solve the well-known clustering problem. The procedure follows a simple and easy way to classify a given data set through a certain number of clusters (assume k clusters) fixed a priori. The main idea is to define k centroids, one for each cluster. These centroids should be placed in a cunning way because of different location causes different result. So, the better choice is to place them as much as possible far away from each other. The next step is to take each point belonging to a given data set and associate it to the nearest centroid. When no point is pending, the first step is completed and an early groupage is done. At this point we need to recalculate k new centroids as bary centers of the clusters resulting from the previous step. After we have these k new centroids, a new binding has to be done between the same data set points and the nearest new centroid. A loop has been generated. As a result of this loop we may notice that the k centroids change their location step by step until no more changes are done. In other words, centroids do not move any more. Finally, this algorithm aims at minimizing an objective function, in this case a squared error function. The objective function where center is a chosen distance measure between a data point and the cluster is an indicator of the distance of the n data points from their respective cluster. The algorithm is composed of the following steps:

i. Place K points into the space represented by the objects that are being clustered. These points represent initial group centroids.
ii. Assign each object to the group that has the closest centroid.
iii. When all objects have been assigned, recalculate the positions of the K centroids.
iv. Repeat Steps 2 and 3 until the centroids no longer move. This produces a separation of the objects into groups from which the metric to be minimized can be calculated.

Although it can be proved that the procedure will always terminate, the k-means algorithm does not necessarily find the most optimal configuration, corresponding to the global objective function minimum. The algorithm is also significantly sensitive to the initial randomly selected cluster centres. The k-means algorithm can be run multiple times to reduce this effect.

9.5 Methodology

As the objective of the project is to improve availability and reduce the wastage of blood stocks due to expiration, a model has been created for the same. In the model, the data given are the demand data of the previous 2+ years, current available blood units as well as their age at any particular blood bank of that State and distance of each blood bank to another blood bank. With this given data, Using time series forecasting, we are applying exponential smoothing method demand for the next week is being forecasted as well as the minimum stock level and maximum stock level to keep at the blood bank is calculated based on the demand data. The available stock at any blood bank will be excess subtracted by the minimum stock. This available stock can be transferred to the blood banks where there is scarcity of stock. A distance matrix is created between all the blood banks of a region. Using K-means clustering algorithm, clusters are formed with centroid k = no. of blood bank with positive availability of blood units to transfer to the blood banks with scarcity. Data containing the emergency level and the quantity of blood units of the particular blood group required in that blood bank is analyzed and then based on the high emergency level the blood units are sent to that blood bank. For transporting the blood units, FIFO and LIFO policies are considered to decide which blood unit with what age is to be sent. After going through literature reviews, it is decided to take a threshold of 14 days age. In this case, we are considering the RBC's whose shelf life is 42 days. If a demand arises then first the oldest blood below 14 days age is sent first. If there are no blood units available then the youngest blood unit above 14 days threshold is sent first. If the requirement is fulfilled by the closest blood bank with availability then the remaining available quantities are sent to the next blood bank with the lesser emergency level. However, if the demand is not fulfilled by the closest blood bank as it goes out of stock then clusters are formed again to fulfill the requirement. The step by step procedure is as follows:

Step 1: Forecast the demand for Month i
Previous year demand data is used to forecast the demand for the next month. Exponential smoothing method is used to do so. The forecasted demand (Fi) for month i is found.
Step 2: Availability (Ak) = Present stock − Min_Stock level
Availability of the blood stock at each blood bank (k) is calculated.
Step 3: Distance Matrix [Dkj] is created between the blood banks.
Step 4: Number of centroids = Number of Blood Banks with Ak > 0
Clustering of the closest banks to the centroid bank is done based on the distance matrix.
Step 5: Emergency level (Ej) and Demand (dj) at blood bank j is analyzed. Max {Ej} is given first priority and processed first.
Step 6:
If dj = Ak {Transfer stock = dj from blood bank k to j}
If dj < Ak {Transfer stock = dj from blood bank k to j
And Repeat steps 2–6}

Step 7:
If dj > Ak{Transfer stock = Ak from blood bank *k*(new) to *j*
Repeat steps 2–5
If dj = Ak (new) Transfer stock = dj − Ak (old) from blood bank *k*(new) to *j*
If dj < Ak (new) Transfer stock = dj − Ak (old) from blood bank *k*(new) to *j* and
Repeat steps 2–6)
If dj > Ak (new) Repeat Step 7}

9.5.1 Results and Discussions

The initial cluster formed based on the distances between the blood banks and the centroid being the blood banks with positive availability of the blood units as shown in Fig. 9.2.

The Table 9.1 represents the values that change after every iteration. The blood bank with scarce blood units receives the blood units from the blood banks with excess units based on the emergency level. The objective of the iterations is to increase the availability of the blood units at any given blood bank but also keeping in mind to first fulfill the emergency situation demands.

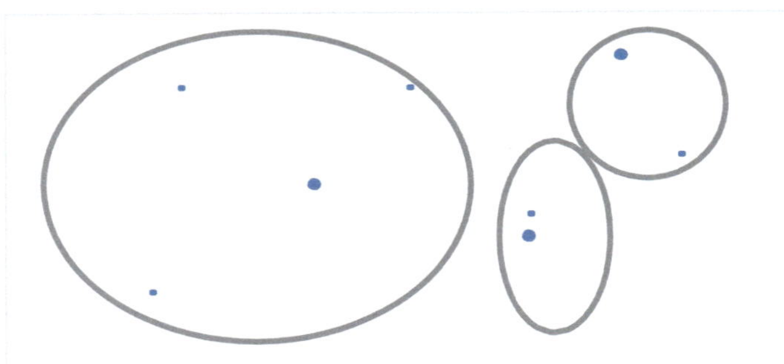

Fig. 9.2 The clusters formed based on the distance matrix at first iteration

Table 9.1 The available blood units after every iteration

Blood Bank	Available Stock after Iterations		
1	117	117	104
2	12	12	12
3	5	5	5
4	73	73	73
5	7	7	20
6	2	24	24
7	54	34	34
8	20	20	20

As can be seen from the above table, in iteration 1, the availability of blood units in blood bank 6 has been increased by 1100%; in iteration 2: The availability of blood units in blood bank 5 has been increased by 185.7%. Also as the blood is a biological product, it cannot be manufactured. It is a deteriorating product, so it is being transferred from the blood banks having excess of blood stocks to reduce the wastage due to expiration. Also, the waiting time is minimum because the distance has been considered to be a crucial factor and considering that in mind the nearest blood banks are coming into action first to supply the extra blood units.

9.6 Summary of Recommendations

The proposed model may be applied to the blood banks of any region. But, there is a problem in forecasting the demand, as it varies from one place to another, so special care should be taken demographically. If the demand is forecasted for a small region, trend and seasonality will hardly be noticeable, but when it is forecasted for a large region it can easily be noticed. The seasonality might occur due to rush during the festival time, election time which causes accidents and thus, demand of blood arises. Trend may be seen, for example, as people suffering from heart diseases increases every year by certain proportions which may increase the demand of blood.

The model is created to solve the real-life problem. A lot of stock goes waste when expired and not taken care when maintained in proper conditions in the inventory. This wastage may be reduced if the excess blood stocks are transferred from these blood banks to the blood banks in scarcity. This problem is prevalent in whole part of India and can be improved when a good information management system is maintained.

9.7 Conclusions

As the objective of the paper is to increase the availability of the blood in any given blood bank by reallocating and redistributing of the blood stocks, decreasing the lead time to reach the demand point from the supply point and reducing the blood stock wastage, an efficient model is created to meet the objective. From the review of the literature, various aspects have been found out. For forecasting the demand, data exponential smoothing method is used as it considers the seasonality and trend in the forecasting. The blood banks with the available blood stock that may be transferred to another blood bank with scarcity is transferred based on the emergency situation at the blood bank in need as well as the distance between the blood banks to reduce the lead time. This has been done by clustering the blood banks using distance matrix. For transporting the blood units, FIFO and LIFO policies are considered to decide which blood unit with what age is to be sent. The model is proved to be efficient as it reallocates the excess stock to the blood banks with scarcity of blood stock. Also, as the clusters are formed using distance matrix the lead time of the blood stock to the blood bank with scarcity is minimum. The data used is randomly generated data as the real-time data from blood bank is confidential and secondary data is unavailable. It would also be interesting to gather real-time data to verify and validate the model. The model may, therefore, be improved with reliable data and further scenario testing continued. Additionally, categorization into blood types may be added to explore the difference in outdating rates for rare blood types versus the common ones. A scenario may be tested to change the age of units that are resent to the centralized stock.

References

Atkinson, M. P., Fontaine, M. J., Goodnough, L. T., & Wein, L. M. (2012). A novel allocation strategy for blood transfusions: Investigating the tradeoff between the age and availability of transfused blood. *Transfusion, 52*(1), 108–117.

Belien, J., & Force, H. (2012). Supply chain management of blood products: A literature review. *European Journal of Operational Research, 217*(1), 1–16.

Brandeau, M. L., Sainfort, F., & Pierskalla, W. P. (2004). *Operations research and health care: A handbook of methods and applications*. Kluwer Academic Publishers.

Croston, J. D. (1972). Forecasting and stock control for intermittent demands. *Operational Research Quarterly, 23*(3), 283–303.

Dillon, M., Oliveirab, F., & Abbasia, B. (2017). A two-stage stochastic programming model for inventory management in the blood supply chain. *International Journal of Production Economics, 187,* 27–41.

Ensafian, H., & Yaghoubi, S. (2017). Robust optimization model for integrated procurement, production and distribution in platelet supply chain. *Transportation Research Part E, 103,* 32–55.

Fahimnia, B., Jabbarzadeh, A., Ghavamifar, A., & Bell, M. (2017). Supply chain design for efficient and effective blood supply in disasters. *International Journal of Production Economics, 183,* 700–709.

Fries, B. (1975). Optimal ordering policy for a perishable commodity with fixed lifetime. *Operations Research, 23*(1), 46–61.

Haijema, R. (2014). Optimal ordering, issuance and disposal policies for inventory management of perishable products. *International Journal of Production Economics, 157,* 158–169.

Hosseinifard, Z., & Abbasi, B. (2016). The inventory centralization impacts on sustainability of the blood supply chain. *Computers & Operations Research*, Article in Press.

Jabbarzadeh, A., Fahimnia, B., & Seuring, S. (2014). Dynamic supply chain network design for the supply of blood in disasters: A robust model with real world application. *Transportation Research Part E, 70,* 225–244.

Omosigho, S. E. (2002). Determination of outdate and shortage quantities in the inventory problem with fixed lifetime. *International Journal Computer Mathematics, 79*(11), 1169–1177.

Pereira, A. (2004). Performance of time-series methods in forecasting the demand for red blood cell transfusion. *Transfusion, 44*(5), 739–746.

Pierskalla, W. P. (2004). Supply chain management of blood banks. In M. L. Brandeau, F. Sainfort, & W. P. Pierskalla (Eds.), *Operations research and health care: A handbook of methods and applications* (p. 103). Kluwer Academic Publishers.

Prastacos, G. P. (1984). Blood inventory management: An overview of theory and practice. *Management Science, 307,* 777–800.

Puranam, K., Novak, D. C., Lucas, M. T., & Fung, M. (2017). Managing blood inventory with multiple independent sources of supply. *European Journal of Operational Research, 259,* 500–511.

Yang, G., & Liu, Y. (2017). Optimizing an equilibrium supply chain network design problem by an improved hybrid biogeography based optimization algorithm. *Applied Soft Computing, 58,* 657–668.

Author Index

P.K. Ray and J. Maiti (eds.), *Healthcare Systems Management: Methodologies and Applications*, Managing the Asian Century,
DOI 10.1007/978-981-10-5631-4

Subject Index

P.K. Ray and J. Maiti (eds.), *Healthcare Systems Management: Methodologies and Applications*, Managing the Asian Century,
DOI 10.1007/978-981-10-5631-4

MIX
Papier aus verantwortungsvollen Quellen
Paper from responsible sources
FSC® C105338

If you have any concerns about our products,
you can contact us on
ProductSafety@springernature.com

In case Publisher is established outside the EU,
the EU authorized representative is:
Springer Nature Customer Service Center GmbH
Europaplatz 3, 69115 Heidelberg, Germany

Printed by Libri Plureos GmbH
in Hamburg, Germany